CW00517165

Turbulence

Turbulence

A Corporate Perspective on Collaborating for Resilience

Edited by
Roland Kupers

Amsterdam University Press

Cover design: Maedium, Utrecht
Typesetting: Crius Group, Hulshout

Amsterdam University Press English-language titles are distributed in the US and Canada by
the University of Chicago Press.

ISBN   978 90 8964 712 2
e-ISBN   978 90 4852 435 8 (pdf)
e-ISBN   978 90 4852 436 5 (ePub)
NUR   800

© Roland Kupers / Amsterdam University Press, Amsterdam 2014

Contents

Part III Resilience in action

Editor's foreword

Roland Kupers

Faced with an increasingly turbulent world and armed with an intuitive insight as to what was driving the turbulence, the CEO's of a group of multinational companies spanning across multiple industries joined forces to explore what their value could and should be in such a changed context.

Turbulence is at the same time familiar and somewhat frightening. Familiar when we dial up the volume on a water tap and the water suddenly no longer flows smoothly. Somewhat frightening when colliding airflows mix and lead to a bumpy flight. Something similar happens in socio-economic systems, interacting with the natural environment.[1] When these systems are tightly coupled, they are likely to stumble across a threshold into turbulent behaviour. Stock markets crash, commodity prices leap, social unrest or extreme weather events occur. The insight the CEOs shared was that the ever-greater demands on food, water and energy systems, in the context of a changing climate, meant that in the future turbulence was likely to become a much more regular feature of the modern world.

In a turbulent world, it would no longer be enough to drive ever-higher economic efficiency and meet ever-more demanding customer needs. Those demands will not go away. What will be added is a requirement to make our socio-economic systems more resilient to the turbulence. To find out what this means and how multinational corporations can contribute, they assembled a project under the banner of the Resilience Action Initiative (RAI). In this book the companies share what they have learnt in their first two years of exploration.

Whenever I have described the story of RAI to people, they have inevitably rushed to the conclusion that the work is only about the resilience of the companies themselves. It is not. Certainly companies need to be resilient, but that is something they worry about continuously and which is part of the core task of management and the board. The premise for RAI is that companies effectively have a societal licence to operate over the long term, but only if they meet a fundamental social need. Cynics may well point to plenty of exceptions, but over time there is little doubt that very large companies are part of society and need to be connected with its long-term requirements. So the focus of RAI is not only on the companies themselves,

1   Scheffer (2009)

but on the resilience of the cities and regions in which they operate and where they eventually sell their products and services. The companies have found that by engaging with the resilience of their environment and that of their clients, they also strengthen their own resilience. As such the two are intimately linked.

This is a book written by practitioners. Most of the authors are senior managers in multinational companies or advisors. As such their prejudice is towards action, rather than towards theory or conceptualisation. This perspective on the resilience of cities and regions is therefore different than what one might find from an NGO or academic perspective. It is not necessarily opposed or in contradiction, but the framing is a corporate framing. This matters because the gap between science and practice – as well as sometimes between NGOs and practice – is often one of framing even though it sometimes is perceived as one of opposed interests. As such, we hope that this book contributes to bridging those gaps by providing a perspective that is less often documented.

The concept of resilience is not new. In the 1970s Buzz Holling was one of its pioneers[2] at the Vienna International Institute for Applied Systems Science (IIASA)[3] where he later became Director. In 1975 Jimmy Davidson, the head of Shell's Group Planning, visited IIASA and concluded that resilience provides the necessary flexibility for societal and ecological systems: "[I]f this flexibility was not possible or if it was too expensive, one had to assess whether the investment was still justified against the risk of not having such flexibility."[4] Resilience cannot be made sense of without the realisation that a system cannot be entirely explained by understanding all its parts. Resilience can only be conceptualised as a property of an interconnected and complex system. These insights are far from new, but a more scientific approach has been catalysed with the founding of the Santa Fe Institute for Complexity Science in 1986. While complexity science itself is in its infancy, its impact on practice can already be felt, in such wide-ranging areas as traffic, epidemiology or public policy.[5]

More recently the Resilience Alliance[6] has connected a network of universities, governments and NGOs. The chair of its board, Brian Walker, has been an advisor to RAI and has written the epilogue to this book.

2   Hollings (1973)
3   http://www.iiasa.ac.at/
4   Quoted in Wilkinson and Kupers (2014)
5   Colander and Kupers (2014)
6   http://www.resalliance.org/

The Rockefeller Foundation has championed multiple initiatives to put resilience into practice, most recently the 100 Resilient Cities initiative[7] that provides direct support and connects resilience strategies in urban areas around the world. Other resilience initiatives are referred to throughout this book, but RAI stands out through its specifically corporate perspective.

Many companies have engaged with the idea of contributing to sustainable development, and the RAI companies have issued various sustainability reports and commitments. As such, the relationship between sustainability and resilience has come up repeatedly. We do not attempt to deal with this in the book, as the focus is resolutely on action, not debating concepts. Suffice it so say here that the two are related. Resilience is more clearly defined as the property of a system with certain dynamic attributes, and as such has more intellectual and practical running room. Sustainability is a powerful and intuitively appealing idea, but one sometimes struggles to add much practicality to it. However, ideas have both emotional, analytical and familiarity appeal, so the point is not deciding whether one concept is better than the other, but what is most effective in each circumstance. Personally, I have favoured resilience as an idea for a long time, as more actionable and more suitable for deepening our understanding.

As much as we live in a world infatuated with 'newness', the reality is that collective human thought moves slowly. It can take decades for an idea to reach the mainstream or to have widespread impact on the practical state of things. Witness ideas such as sustainability or climate mitigation. In the economic realm the validity of concepts such as privatisation, the primacy of shareholder value or market efficiency take time to root, but also wax and wane. For our purpose, we should recall that companies are very large institutions, which also need time to absorb a new idea and work out how it can make a difference in practice. Resilience is not just about *individual* engagement, but *institutional* engagement. While this may seem slow at times, this is what makes it impactful. People will refer to the fact that a particular company is part of their project or involved in their initiative. However, the depth of those kinds of participations can vary immensely and sometimes it is merely a single employee. Companies are large institutions in their own right, and engaging them comprehensively is time consuming, as well as a major effort. The challenge of understanding and designing resilience solutions is one for the long haul, which will require deep engagement of substantial parts of the institutions. Part of the RAI

7   http://100resilientcities.rockefellerfoundation.org/

journey has been and will continue to be to deepen the roots of the idea in the various companies.

The book is structured as follows: After the preface by Peter Voser who took the initiative to convene the Resilience Action Initiative when he was the CEO of Royal Dutch Shell, followed by an introductory remark from Michel Liès, CEO of Swiss Re, Part I of the book contains a single chapter describing the activities and approach of RAI.

In Part II the tools and methods developed by RAI are listed. Chapter 2 contains the simple resilience frame that was developed and fine-tuned to engage project teams and look with them through the resilience lens. Chapter 3 further deepens the tools and applies them to consider how enterprise risk management becomes different in a resilience perspective. Chapter 4 is the result of a workshop convened by IUCN with a grant from the Rockefeller Foundation, which looked at cross-sector collaboration for resilience, and Chapter 5 lists examples for such collaborations and what success factors can be distilled from them.

In Part III aspects of resilience activities are described, ranging from green infrastructure in Chapter 6 and Nexus!, the resilience game developed for RAI, in Chapter 7. Due to the nature of its members as large companies, many of the projects that RAI considered tended to be large scale, so a project to experiment with bottom-up projects for resilience ran in parallel and is described in Chapter 8. Chapter 9 reflects on the first two years of RAI collaboration. Brian Walker, the Chairman of the Resilience Alliance, provides the epilogue.

As much as RAI focused on the challenges of translating the need for resilience into action, it cannot do this without the support of research-ers furthering the science. As a small contribution, the royalties from the sales of this book are donated to the Resilience Alliance to support its research programmes. The contributions of the named authors are made individually, with mention of their affiliations, in the context of an overall corporate collaborative project. Finally, I would like to express thanks to the RAI companies for the privilege of exploring resilience with them,[8] to Brian Walker for being such an inspiring thinking partner to RAI, to the Smith School of Enterprise and the Environment for generously extending Associate Fellow status and to the team at Amsterdam University Press for their support and their ability to publish this book in record time.

---

8   Roland Kupers Consultancy received payments from RAI companies for services during 2012 and 2013.

Preface

Peter Voser

In early 2010, as the multilateral world was still licking its wounds from the disappointing Copenhagen Summit on Climate Change, one of my advisors asked me about the evolving global policy and technology agenda and what Royal Dutch Shell's role as an integrated energy company should be.

In response, I said that we as an innovative company needed to obtain a better understanding of the energy, water, food and climate 'stress nexus' by working in partnership with others across sectors and value chains and focusing on small-scale initiatives rather than grand designs.

That answer was based on the insights I had gained in over two years as CEO of Shell. I had engaged with many political, civil society and industry leaders, and several common themes had emerged. One shared concern was and continues to be the broken circle of trust between government, industry and society. The financial crisis in 2009 unleashed a wave of public scepticism in Western countries about banks and invited a host of policy measures. These measures came with spill-over effects for other sectors, including energy, chemicals and manufacturing. One aspiration I shared with CEOs of other leading industrial companies was to remind society of the importance of industry as a generator of real jobs, a funder of Research & Development and a provider of the energy and products without which modern society cannot exist. We also wanted to demonstrate that the people working in these companies have the talent and the commitment to contribute to society and drive progress on the ground, even in the absence of clear global policy frameworks.

In Asia and the Middle East, the attitude towards the energy sector and industrial enterprises tends to be more positive. Companies like Shell are seen as indispensable partners for fostering development and growth, while addressing the main downsides of development: environmental degradation and resource scarcity. Their key challenge is how to fuel and feed a growing population with energy, food and water against a backdrop of urbanisation and improving living standards.

Meanwhile, in Shell, our own experts were indicating that the water-energy nexus was going to be absolutely vital for going forward, either as a fundamental challenge or as a critical success factor, depending on how Shell as a company would respond: it takes water to produce and process energy; it takes energy to produce, treat and transport water; and it takes both energy and water to produce food. We saw that the water-energy nexus was going to make itself especially felt in arid regions with growing populations like the Middle East and North Africa.

The 2010 conversations were the beginning of a new phase of strategic thinking to broaden the company's understanding of the linkages and stresses in the world's energy, food and water systems, to identify key factors that make companies, cities and countries resilient in the face of these stresses, and, finally, to build partnerships to drive progress in these areas.

Shell's New Lens Scenarios, published in 2013, included more thinking on energy-water-food, resilience and urbanisation than ever before. The scenarios were built on several years of joint research with academic institutions and think tanks. We included water data in Shell's World Energy Model, so that Shell's scenario team can now factor both CO_2 pricing and water constraints into their modelling, thus contributing to the long-term resilience of the company.

Working on solutions to address the nexus and increase systemic resilience require new ways of working, as these complex challenges cross boundaries between countries, industries as well as the public and private sectors. Solving them requires a broad, holistic approach, an open mind and an understanding beyond our own areas of expertise.

To further foster systemic thinking and collaboration, I convened a small group of chief executives from a number of different sectors. We wanted to show that big corporations can make progress even if there is no pressure from government and civil society to do so. We were like-minded CEOs of companies that face similar or similar-scale challenges. We quickly found that mayors of cities are natural partners to CEOs, since their problems are just as concrete and their solutions have to be just as real. And we like to work together with NGOs such as The Nature Conservancy (TNC), Wetlands International, International Union for the Conservation of Nature (IUCN) or the World Resources Institute (WRI) that have the capacity and will to look beyond single issues and deal with complexity.

The first CEO meeting was held in Davos in early 2012 and brought together CEOs with a personal passion, a long-term vision, and a willingness to drive progress personally from the top. This meeting in Davos led to the creation of the 'Resilience Action Initiative'. Since then, we have made progress, made mistakes and learned a lot. The rest of this book serves as testimony.

For CEOs interested in driving progress in areas that are unexplored and where progress cannot be measured in next year's shareholder returns, I have some tips:

- Build your narrative carefully and gradually. Don't give the whole story too early if you can't make a link to foreseeable benefits. You will need to use lots of psychology.
- Show resilience as a leader – keep pushing it through until key leaders and staff are convinced. At Shell, it took two years, and now senior Shell leaders in critical areas of the company are deploying systemic thinking and resilience methodology in different areas of operation.
- Small pilot projects can be difficult to set up and finish, but they are good for inspiration and encouragement and for creating feedback loops with knowledge work streams.
- Embed new ways of thinking in your overall innovation drive and make clear innovation goes beyond technology.
- Promote integration of thought leadership in these new areas with the brand expressions your people are already familiar with – the synergies will surprise and inspire your people and help you to overcome resistance. (For instance, at Shell, we developed close integration between our resilience work streams and the Shell Eco-marathon and Shell Powering Progress Together events.)
- Finally, be a collaborative leader, which means having the curiosity and willingness to learn, the humility to work with partners whose skills and capabilities complement your own, and the sense to be practical and action-oriented.

Looking back at my years as a leader at Shell, I am more convinced than ever that effective leadership is about having the right balance between focus and vision. It's not an easy balance to achieve or maintain. The leader of an industrial company that aspires to be competitive had better stay focused on the company's core skills and capabilities. At the same time, one needs to have the societal antenna to position the company in the cycle of major policy and technology trends, so it can help shape them. The stress nexus is going to be with us for decades to come, as will be the search for resilience. This search will require closer cooperation between companies, cities and NGOs than ever before in modern corporate history. It is satisfying to know that the Resilience Action Initiative has given its member companies a chance to dip into the future and position themselves as active and innovative players, rather than as passive bystanders.

Peter Voser, The Hague, May 2014

Turbulence – by way of an introduction

Michel Liès

Sipping a cup of tea during a flight through blue skies is easy. If stormy weathers bring about considerable air turbulence, this simple task rapidly becomes pretty difficult. Clouds announce a storm – hence one can prepare and safely stow the cup away in due time. But what if there are no visible early warning signs, as is the case with clear–air turbulence? And what if turbulence prevails? When will be the next chance to take a sip of tea again?

Such are the challenges for a global economy, which has grown fast for decades, providing wealth and more favourable conditions to ever more people. Stresses in critical sectors such as water, energy and food increase. These three sectors are inextricably linked, and changes in one area very often impact one or both of the others. The respective resources form a nexus which itself is affected by external factors such as a growing population, changing economies, international trade, governance issues, health impacts, environmental degradation, and climate change. This high level of interconnectedness and the growing scarcity of resources will likely lead to prolonged times of turbulence – and their onset will be ever harder to predict.

Holding steady despite of turbulence might still work for some time– but resisting change will come at an ever higher cost, possibly until it is too late to change at all. Much better it seems to be to navigate turbulent waters in a more adaptive fashion, guided both by foresight and flexibility.

There are at least three elements that need to be present in order to do so: the willingness to collaborate, a shared vision, and a conceptual frame to integrate required actions. The concept of resilience lends itself to fostering concerted action and hence provides such a frame. Resilience is understood here to be the capacity of business, economic and social structures to survive, adapt, and grow in the face of change and uncertainty related to disturbances, whether they be caused by resource stresses, societal stresses and/or acute events.

A more resilient approach does not come for free – in fact costs will appear high compared to what the continuation of an assumedly a steady world would require. But with increasing levels and/or persistence of turbulence, benefits will outweigh costs. Hence a resilient approach will turn out to be the most economic one – for those who are in for the long run, at least.

Looking into a specific case, namely how to strengthen disaster risk resilience in the face of climate change, decision makers need facts to start with: Not only do they need to know the potential climate-related damage over the coming decades, but also how these risks can best be managed, what measures need to be taken. They also need to know what investment will be required to fund those measures – and whether the benefits will outweigh the costs over time.

When studying the situation along the US Gulf coast, we learned that losses related to hurricane risk will increase substantially in the coming decades. The primary driver will be economic development, with the situation likely further aggravated by climate change. The good news is that a substantial amount of the risk can be cost-effectively averted. This does not come for free, but will nevertheless be far cheaper than bearing the cost of future damages. Investments in risk prevention and preparedness are complemented by risk transfer solutions designed to cope with low frequency/high severity events. Insurance puts a price tag on risks, hence provides risk transparency. This helps decision makers to internalise known externalities, even future ones, such as climate change impacts – and in addition, such a price tag incentivises preventive action.

Decision makers are thus enabled to integrate adaptation with economic development and sustainable growth. Commercial players in the Gulf region further realised that the earlier and more deeply they engage with the communities they serve, the better off both their customers and they themselves are – hence building the case to strengthen societal resilience.

In the context of the present book, we have expanded on such findings, since their relevance and effectiveness strongly depends on the character of the specific company and the environment in which it is embedded. By introducing a wider concept for enterprise resilience, we hope to provide practitioners well beyond the risk community with a novel and practical approach, namely the companies' opportunity to look at their challenges through a series of *resilience lenses*.

Admittedly, in many areas, there are trade-offs between short-term efficiency and long-term resilience. But instead of waiting for the occasional shock to reveal whether enough responsive diversity is in place, the resilience lenses described in this book can be used to identify adequate levels of modularity and redundancy.

Such modular and redundant control systems are at work in airplanes, but more is needed to keep planes flying. Pilots do not fly in isolation. They are in regular contact with air traffic control and are provided with meteorological forecasts. This way, clear–air turbulence can be anticipated in the cockpit – and experienced turbulence is reported back. While weather matters for the single flight, thinking on longer timescales is required for the airline and its fleet: What destinations will be served, which technology will propel the planes, what stresses will need to be coped with? To answer these questions, forecasts will not be enough. Scenarios help to test the resilience of strategies for actors to navigate the unknown. In this context, continuous experimentation and innovation allow a company to learn faster. This increases adaptive capacity – to develop emergent responses in turbulent times.

Michel Liès, Zürich, May 2014
Group CEO, Swiss Re

Part I
Introduction to RAI

1   The Resilience action initiative: An introduction

Maike Böggemann[1] and Norbert Both[2]

At first glance, large multinational companies such as Dow, DuPont, IBM, Royal Dutch Shell, Siemens and Swiss Re are resilient companies: they each have been around for over a century. But the future is volatile. The challenge these companies face today is how to help strengthen societal resilience in the face of increasing systemic turbulence caused by resource and environmental stresses – posing new risks to business continuity and therefore to their existence over the next 100 years.

These companies share a belief that the resilience lens can help. Resilience is the ability to absorb disturbances, to change, to reorganise, and to learn from them at the same time. Resilience thinking goes beyond traditional risk management. It also prepares a society or a company for systemic changes or unforeseen events. The financial crisis of 2008 is an example. How likely is a crisis of this magnitude to reoccur, or should policy focus instead on increasing the systemic resilience for such shocks?

A major challenge for countries and companies is the security of global energy supply. The world needs to increase energy supplies for a growing and more prosperous population. This in itself will put the resilience of the energy system to the test. Because of the stresses on resources like energy, water and food – augmented by their interconnectivity and climate change – the world also faces an enormous systemic challenge. Growing prosperity can lead to stresses – environmental, political and social – that can undermine some of the benefits of prosperity.

The interconnections are complex, and there is an urgent need to understand these connections and formulate answers. This is a collaborative task, with the dual aim of building society's resilience and corporate resilience.

With the aim to improve understanding of the nexus, drive thinking on resilience, and test ideas on the ground in pilot projects and operations, the CEOs of a number of companies[3] came together in Davos in January 2012

---

1   Project Manager, Strategy & Scenarios, Shell.
2   VP Corporate Communications, Shell.
3   Dow, Dupont, IBM, McKinsey & Company, Rio Tinto, Royal Dutch Shell, Siemens, Swiss Re, Unilever; Yara joined subsequently and Rio Tinto left the group.

and agreed to launch a joint project to explore these questions together: the Resilience Action Initiative.

Understanding the 'stress nexus'

In the decades ahead, as the world's population continues to grow, the middle class continues to expand, and more people choose to live in ever-larger cities, the stresses on global energy, water and food systems will become critical.

Every day, the number of people inhabiting our planet grows by more than 210,000. That adds up to 1.5 million more people each and every week, adding to the demands on our vital resources. At the same time, the world is becoming more prosperous, improving the quality of life almost everywhere. Over the past few decades, an estimated two billion people worldwide have attained a level of income to afford a middle-class lifestyle. That is a remarkable achievement.

By 2030, according to the United Nations and Shell's Business Environment (Scenario) team,[4] it is estimated that our world will need between 30% and 50% more water, energy and food to keep up with rising demand. And we will need to provide that additional energy, water, and food in ways that significantly reduce CO_2 emissions.

Addressing any of these resource needs individually would be an immense task. But the challenge of ensuring sufficient supplies of water, energy and food is magnified many times by the linkages between them. The potential effects of climate change will influence all three. So, if we are to succeed in meeting our resource needs, these must be addressed intelligently and holistically.

Energy, water and food are our most vital resources, sustaining life itself and fuelling our modern societies. And they comprise a tightly intertwined network: nearly all forms of energy production require water; energy also is needed to move and treat water; and producing food requires both energy and water.

Yet, around the world, little has been done to address our needs in a comprehensive way. Inefficient resource use remains the norm. In developing countries – where most of the world's population growth is occurring – sound water management is lacking, and up to 40% of electricity is lost due to poor transmission infrastructure. In the developed world, waste is

4   Shell (2013)

also prevalent: more than one-third of the food produced in the United States goes uneaten, for example.

At the same time, we live in an era of greater economic volatility. This, in turn, is generating more political volatility, which tends to impede progress on large-scale global issues. In response, we need to learn to adapt our resource systems and institutions to deal with the new pace of change and uncertainty.

Against this background, in 2011 Shell's CEO Peter Voser launched a new phase of strategic thinking to broaden the company's understanding of the growing stresses and linkages at the nexus of energy, food and water systems.

To better understand this nexus, Shell's scenario team brought together academics and experts from industry, government and non-governmental organisations in 2011. Against this background, one of the authors, Maike, began to highlight within Shell the increasing strategic significance of water beyond the operational importance that had long been understood and addressed. Independently, the head of Shell scenarios, Jeremy Bentham, was considering how to refresh and stretch thinking about environmental matters in the company and was introduced by Johan Rockström to his work on Planetary Boundaries through a cross-sector workshop at the Tällberg Forum. Recognising that key features of the scientific planetary boundaries analysis could be expressed in terms of water security, energy security and food security that would be more compelling to a wider audience, the convergence of insights from Maike and Jeremy led to further Shell attention. In 2011 the Shell scenario team brought together academics and experts from industry, government and non-governmental organisations to consider the nexus collectively, and at this gathering the other author of this chapter, Norbert, recognised the immediate significance of the topic for the CEO. So, in 2011 Shell's CEO Peter Voser also became a champion of this issue and launched a new phase of strategic thinking to broaden the company's understanding of the Nexus of energy, food, and water systems. This included a large exercise to map the nexus, working with Dr Eric Berlow, an expert in complexity science at the University of California, Berkeley. The aim was to look at the complex relationships of the nexus to establish whether a subset of critical issues emerges – disproportionately strong levers that merit targeted efforts and investments.

The work highlighted two main levers: sustainable urban development and greenhouse gas emissions regulation and carbon pricing. For example, designing smarter, energy-efficient cities could help reduce demand for energy and water. Such cities would integrate transport, energy, water and waste systems much more effectively than today's cities.

And greenhouse gas emissions regulation can spur more energy-efficient behaviours and technology deployment. Without such regulation, climate change could have a significant impact on dry regions becoming drier, agriculture being impacted and even more people moving into cities.

The Resilience Action Initiative

Clearly, these complex challenges cross boundaries between countries, industries and the public and private sectors and solving them will require a broad, holistic approach, an open mind and an understanding beyond our own areas of expertise.

This is why collaboration is so critical. It is the only way we can create new systems and approaches to foster growth in ways that mitigate these global stresses in a resource-constrained world.

In the context of the energy-water-food nexus, it means businesses, NGOs and governments joining forces to find comprehensive solutions. For instance, Shell currently has formal collaborative partnerships with select environmental NGOs at a strategic and operational level. Shell works with the International Union for the Conservation of Nature (IUCN), Wetlands International, Earthwatch and The Nature Conservancy to improve its energy projects in terms of reducing its environmental footprint and increase positive impact on communities.

In late 2011, Peter Voser convened a small group of business leaders from different sectors to find ways of working together to advance knowledge and increase experience with a view to making society more resilient in the face of growing resource and environmental strains. Letters went out and in January 2012, at the World Economic Forum in Davos, leaders of Dow, DuPont, Rio Tinto, McKinsey & Co., IBM, Unilever, Shell and Siemens came together to discuss the merits of cooperation. In the ensuing months, the Swiss re-insurer Swiss Re and the Norwegian fertiliser company Yara also joined.

The outcome of this meeting was an initiative later called the Resilience Action Initiative (RAI) with the vision of supporting more resilient economies at the levels of regions, cities and industrial clusters. To achieve the vision, RAI would explore collaborative business models and open platforms that could measurably contribute to increased system resilience. Over the course of the next few months a number of work streams were created, some focused on enhancing methodology, others on driving action on the ground.

This initiative differed from previous approaches in that it was strictly corporate, not imposed by law or triggered by stakeholder pressure. Voser and like-minded CEOs like Dow's Andrew Liveris, and DuPont's Ellen Kullman wanted to put some distance between their companies and a financial sector-induced crisis of confidence in the capitalist world, and reclaim the industrial sector's rightful place at the heart of society.

Definition of resilience

With the dramatic increase in computing power at the back end of the 20th century a new field of knowledge emerged: complexity science. It explores how complex systems behave and how they respond to stresses. Resilience is a property of a complex system – it is the capacity to survive, adapt and grow in the face of change and uncertainty, particularly related to disturbances with a high impact and low probability. It is a property of any complex system, be it your body, a company, a sector, a city, a country.

Unlike sustainability, it has no normative connotation. A drug cartel or a nasty virus can be very resilient. More resilience therefore is not always a good thing. To achieve change, a (temporary) reduction of resilience may be needed. When considering resilience, it is necessary to always answer the question, "The resilience of what, against which stresses?"

Various resilience experts and commentators have noted that the RAI companies' focus on resilience as a theme was relevant, timely and ambitious, with answers to resilience questions far from obvious.

Indeed, RAI proved to be more a journey of discovery and learning, which continues today, than it was a readily implementable action plan. While the imperative to address the resilience of natural as well as socio-economic systems is beyond doubt, the way to go about it is only partially clear. Science is only starting to learn what determines system resilience.

One can define resilience as a concept in different ways. For RAI effort, the companies settled on: *Resilience is the capacity of business, economic and social structures to survive, adapt and grow in the face of change and uncertainty related to disturbances, whether they be caused by resource stresses, societal stresses and/or acute events.*

Thus far resilience had been relatively unexplored in the natural resources and socio-economic domain. Over the last two years the theme has gained prominence in government, business and civil society – particularly in bringing the interests of different stakeholders closer together. It is a powerful lens for the contribution the private sector makes to society as well as the environment society creates for thriving business. Furthermore, all resilient systems – be it an organisation, a city or a river basin – share certain characteristics. Resilience concepts are complementary to traditional risk management approaches and useful when thinking about adaptation and transformation in the face of change and uncertainty.

Resilience can be considered in relation to risk management. Risk management is traditionally a fairly linear process of listing the internal and external risks to achieving an objective, and identifying measures to eliminate the risk or mitigate the impact. The quality of risk management clearly depends heavily on the competencies of the people involved and may already have elements of resilience incorporated.

Resilience thinking and dialogue enhances risk management practices. It promotes an understanding of how risks are interlinked but moreover it is about understanding and enhancing those properties of a system that make it inherently more resilient, also to unidentified risks. A distinction is made between *specific* and *generic* resilience. Specific resilience is resilience against a particular known risk or stress, e.g. the capacity of New York City to deal with the next Superstorm Sandy. Generic resilience is the capacity of a system to deal with many different kinds of stresses, including those that are unknown.

The RAI approach

The RAI programme has consisted of different types of activities:
– Knowledge projects
– On-the-ground engagements and pilots, and bottom-up initiatives
– Broader sharing and dialogue

The programme was coordinated by a global working group with representatives from all RAI companies. The working group members engaged their own organisations and networks in the programme.

The approach agreed by RAI companies was to develop the methodology in parallel with the pilots, and not sequentially. In this way, the pilots' experiences influenced the methodology development. At the same time, the engagements on the ground were able to use elements of the methodology at various stages of its development.

The knowledge projects were aimed at understanding resilience, understanding how corporates and others contribute to resilience, what resilience means to an organisation, what different forms collaborations for resilience can take, why collaborations for resilience can struggle and what can make them successful. They were typically led by one of the RAI members with other members contributing expertise and case studies from their own organisations and initiatives. Furthermore, a network of academics from around the world, all engaged in different sciences related to resilience, contributed their perspectives and a scientific view on the challenge.

Thinking about resilience is a challenge in itself, but working in practice is possibly as, if not more, difficult. The on-the-ground engagements and pilots were meant to test and inform the thinking and give a real sense of the challenges. In the on-the-ground engagements we have worked on different complex systems – a city, an industrial cluster, a watershed, a country – to learn what resilience means in different geographies and scales. Also we have tried to focus on different subsystems – water, energy, food, transport, waste – to increase our shared understanding of resilience on different issues and their interdependencies. In the beginning these engagements were very exploratory, as the thinking had not matured. Often they felt uncomfortable as specific objectives and expectations were opaque. There was hesitation driven by a feeling of inadequacy because we did not really know what we were doing and a high risk of investing time and relationships for an uncertain return.

Inspired by a desire to complement the CEO-led approach, and to engage and inspire young people and leverage their different set of capabilities, an effort was made to facilitate young professionals from the RAI companies as well as public and civil society organisations to come together to have an impact on the ground through tangible actions. The appetite to work together, the passion with which these young professionals dedicated (often personal) time to the effort, and the hands-on creativity they brought were remarkable. Chapter 8 further details this approach and its initial results.

Broader sharing and dialogue is important to involve a critical mass of individuals and organisations in the thinking and inspire them to act together. We have found that the resilience frame of mind takes some time to adjust to, and requires some real experience to fully understand. To provide for an efficient and fun introduction to the topic, the nexus and resilience knowledge work was translated into a board game. The game has been played with CEOs, mayors, scientists, members of NGOs and students. It is described in Chapter 7. Furthermore, various workshops were organised and attended by RAI members to do so. During the programme a broad network of individuals and organisations with an interest in resilience developed.

The two-year journey was intensive and required a great deal of personal resilience from all involved. Every few months existential challenges were raised and the scope, way of working and thinking would be updated after working through our insecurities. The open challenge and collaboration developed a significant trust base between the individuals and teams involved.

Knowledge projects

The knowledge projects in 2011 focused on a 'methodology and framework for improving resilience' and 'green infrastructure'. In 2012 further projects looked at the topics of 'collaboration models and success factors' and 'resilience in relation to (enterprise) risk management'.

The *methodology* work explored ways in which resilience can be approached, discussed and improved. Its aim has been to develop a process and toolkit. As resilience challenges are inherently complex it serves as a useful handrail for aligning stakeholders in a collaborative effort on a process and guiding the dialogue. It was developed in several stages and re-assessed with the lessons from the on-the-ground engagements and pilots. This work is described in the following chapter.

Green infrastructure solutions integrate value and risk assessment across different parts of the nexus. Biological systems, in contrast with engineered systems, are generally more compatible with a resilience perspective. The focus of the green infrastructure knowledge workstream was sharing best practices and identifying tools, approaches and barriers that would improve the ability of companies to consider, evaluate and implement 'green infrastructure' options in addition to or instead of traditional 'grey infrastructure' choices. 'Green infrastructure' can be defined as the use of natural ecosystems to provide a service that is often provided by traditional 'grey infrastructure' engineering solutions. For example, protection from floods and storms can often be accomplished by levees, but can also be accomplished via the use of wetlands and coastal marshes in place of and/ or in addition to levees. In many cases, 'green infrastructure' solutions can provide not only the same functionality as the 'grey infrastructure' alternative, but usually also provide valuable co-benefits to ecosystems and are more cost-effective. Chapter 6 lists a number of examples of green infrastructure and what the barriers are to scaling up such solutions.

In the RAI journey we discussed and re-evaluated the RAI operating model at many stages, which led to the realisation that different *collaboration* models exist and are useful for different objectives. It also became clear that collaborations often struggle and there was a desire to understand better why that is the case and which ingredients can add to the success of collaborations. A broad review was done on multiple existing collaborative projects and lessons on structure and critical enablers were extracted. The broadening of the RAI agenda to include multiple stakeholders culminated in a conference hosted at the Rockefeller Foundation's Bellagio Centre, and organised by the International Union for the Conservation of Nature (IUCN). This work is elaborated on in Chapter 3 and Chapter 4.

What began as a translation of the resilience thinking in corporate terms, *relating it to enterprise risk management,* grew to become a framework for examining properties of any system which can increase its resilience, and where resilience properties require balancing or trade-offs with other organisational objectives. It furthermore explores the role of generic resilience, the resilience of a complex system to yet unknown stresses. This work is covered in Chapter 5.

The challenges of resilience in practice

The on-the-ground engagements and pilots have generated great interest among local government and other stakeholders to engage with the RAI partners on resilience. The focus in the pilots differs by location.

Da Nang, a major port city in Vietnam, was the first location where RAI engaged with a city government. The aim of the engagement was to explore options for the city to enhance its ability to adapt to and to recover successfully from acute threats such as floods and earthquakes, chronic threats such as constrained energy supplies and unanticipated threats such as political transitions and economic transformations. The pilot covered several issues like water, transportation, energy and economic development and produced recommendations on integrated water management and food safety.

In *Rotterdam*, the second-largest city in the Netherlands and one of the largest ports in the world, the resilience of the port and its relation with the city were subject of an ongoing dialogue between RAI and public stakeholders. Particularly the challenges of a delta-city and the interconnection between the municipality and the port were discussed. Subsequently, Rotterdam was selected as one of the 100 resilient cities in the Rockefeller Foundation programme and will continue to explore resilience as an opportunity.

To develop energy resilience, RAI members shared best practice as most had quite some experience with energy efficiency within their own operations, or working with suppliers and customers on their energy efficiency. From initial sharing of best practice it became clear that a relatively unexplored area of opportunity is improving the energy efficiency within a geographic industrial cluster and possibly with a neighbouring city. The impediments for integration in an industrial cluster were identified not as lack of technology solutions but rather the lack of data sharing, agency issues (risk-reward balance) and the lack of proven business and financing models. The members decided to explore this opportunity for resilience through an energy resilience pilot at Jurong Island in *Singapore*. The McKinsey Green Campus (a small-scale refinery turned into an energy-efficiency training facility on Jurong Island) served as the base for this exploration of the opportunity to improve the overall utility (power, heat, steam) efficiency and resilience on Jurong Island by improving the connections between neighbouring companies' data, people and assets.

A multi-stakeholder dialogue in *Houston* has led to multiple collaborative efforts in the areas of waste-to-energy and lowering CO_2 emissions from transport. For example 'Houston Flows' is a project seeks to help reduce the environmental footprint from the transportation of people, goods, and services within and through the Greater Houston Area, which currently account for over 40% of the City of Houston's GHG emissions. One component being explored is to drive behavioral changes that help create more sustainable mobility choices by Shell Houston employees within and across facilities.

In a multi-year programme in *South Africa* RAI members have brought together a broad group of global and national, public, private and civil society organisations to better understand the country's nexus, resilience challenges and policy options. One of the topics is the collaboration between sectors to be more resilient to water stress and the policy environment that is a critical enabler for cross-sector collaboration. In an on-the-ground pilot in a watershed the insights from the national engagement are tested.

Bottom-up initiatives by young professionals from different organisations coming together have led to 'real action' and spin-off business in *Rotterdam* and *South Africa* on urban farming and ecosystem restoration. Further initiatives are underway in *Manila*, *Groningen* and *Nigeria*.

It is fair and important to note that some initiatives did not take off and many initiatives developed at a much slower pace than expected. A significant amount of time and effort was invested in building trust. Sometimes it was difficult to identify shared interests that were a priority to the partners in the collaboration. Often it was a challenge to not let one's own organisation's short-term interests undermine the collaborative effort.

Broader sharing and dialogue

Some of the RAI knowledge work has also been captured in Nexus!, the RAI resilience game. This is a fast-paced, interactive resource development and trading board game aimed at letting participants experience the linkages between resources in the nexus, resilience strategies and collaboration challenges. To date, the game has been played by over 2000 participants from students to executives, public authorities, NGO representatives and academics. Developing awareness and promoting systemic thinking is a critical part of the journey.

RAI members through organising and attending multiple conferences around the world have also promoted broader dialogue.

RAI has been a vehicle for exploring resilience, however, there are many more initiatives to improve resilience outside RAI, including ones that have emerged from business activities. To quote but two examples of many:

– Canada's Oil Sands Innovation Alliance (COSIA)[5] is a collaborative effort between leading oil sands producers to rapidly accelerate environmental performance. Sharing research, knowledge and expertise between 14 industry companies, COSIA minimises barriers and drives the discovery and development of environmental innovations, solutions and best practices throughout the oil sands. The COSIA model is being expanded to non-oil sands company members, in an 'Associate Membership Programme'. The intent of the programme is to harness the vast leveraging potential from a wide range of members from engineering firms, to universities, governments etc. In just a year since startup, over 440 technologies or innovations have been contributed by the member companies, with development costs over $700 million.

– The Center for Sustainable Shale Development (CSSD)[6] in Pennsylvania, USA, has developed performance standards for shale gas production development and a commitment to continuous improvement to ensure safe and environmentally responsible development of the abundant shale resources. CSSD is an unprecedented collaboration built on constructive engagement among environmental organisations, philanthropic foundations and energy companies from across the Appalachian Basin.

Collaboration and leadership

While resilience is a concept people can intuitively relate to, it is also a mindset change. It needs an outside-in perspective, a systemic view on how the resilience of the environment in which you work impacts you,

5   http://www.cosia.ca/
6   http://www.sustainableshale.org/

and in turn, how you contribute to the resilience of the environment in which you operate. It demands a deep insight into the interdependencies of success. Resilience in the complex systems of society we work in cannot be achieved without collaboration as it always crosses organisational, sectoral and geographical boundaries.

When there is a shared understanding of our interdependencies, a dialogue about resilience of the broader system we all are a part of can facilitate bringing different stakeholders closer together and identifying where interests are aligned. This cannot be achieved without strong and authentic leadership, a leadership that fundamentally recognises and values interdependencies as core assets to protect and enhance value. Shell explored the role of leadership in collaborations at the energy-water-food nexus together with consulting firm Xynteo.[7]

In all of these collaborations leadership is critical. Experience shows that collaborations of this kind tend to struggle for a number of reasons, including the fact that sectors are not used to working together. But if leaders put in place and follow a proper process, collaboration has the potential to unlock latent value that resides at the interface between the sectors, boosting growth and adapting to the challenges. Achieving this requires a new kind of leadership – one that brings people to the table and, despite the inevitable challenges, keeps them there. With no hierarchy, and people participating as peers, traditional 'top-down' styles of leadership are ill-suited to collaboration.

Collaborative leaders are different. They instead inspire partners to commit to a common narrative, and then forge, promote and protect a collaborative process that catalyses action between the partners. They empower and enable collaborative partners to carry it out. This demands a distinct set of behaviours. First, collaborative leaders need to be able to move beyond a perspective of pure self-interest to putting the interests of the collaboration in front. Second, collaborative leaders, whose primary role is to serve the partners, need to involve others in the process to get their buy-in as well as ensuring that the best solution is tabled, while maintaining a decisive hand to keep partners within the process. To behave in such a way, collaborative leaders, unlike with a traditional leadership style, need to be comfortable with releasing control of the situation. This may require collaborative leaders to remove a number of personal barriers, such as ego, defensiveness and a desire for power, that are preventing them from inspiring commitment and catalysing action. Not an easy feat.

7   http://www.xynteo.com/

Part II
The resilience lens

2   A pragmatic frame to explore resilience

Marco Albani[1] and Roland Kupers[2]

In a world faced with increasing volatility and turbulence, business leaders find the idea of working to bolster the resilience of the economic systems in which they operate both attractive and intuitive. Yet we found that operationalising this idea is quite difficult, and it is especially difficult to do so in a way that fully captures the richness of perspective that resilience and complexity sciences have developed over the last four decades.

The complexity stems from the fact that resilience is an emergent property of complex systems that is revealed in the face of uncertain events, and as such is very hard to measure, especially *ex ante*. Adaptive capacity is the prime capability associated with resilience, encompassing the abilities to rapidly exploit new opportunities, manage complex and interconnected systems, and read and respond to signals of change.[3] This adaptive capacity can appear either like change or stasis. In a corporate world, resilience can take the form of Shell still operating in the same main markets after a century or of IBM reinventing itself several times – both are successful, and hence resilient in their own right.

So while the concept is intuitive and appealing, and can be compellingly discussed at the conceptual level, there is a real challenge in moving from the conceptual to the practical without falling in the trap of reverting to traditional risk management approaches, which are certainly useful, but often do not capture the richness of insight that a resilience lens could bring to bear. For example, Value at Risk (VaR) calculations assume that risk distributions are *normal*, an assumption that is often invalid for the tightly coupled complex systems for which the resilience frame is developed. In fact, most systems for which we will be interested in their resilience, have *non-normal* risk distributions with fat tails (or black swans) that undermine the very essence of the standard risk management tools.

In our work with the Resilience Action Initiative (RAI), we found the need to develop a simple resilience frame that can be used to move from the conceptual to the practical, while retaining as much of the richness

1   Senior Expert, Sustainability and Resource Productivity Practice of McKinsey & Company.
2   Associate Fellow, the Smith School of Enterprise and the Environment, University of Oxford.
3   Reeves and Deimler (2011)

of insight and approach developed through resilience science as possible. We developed this frame, which we will describe in the next section, to facilitate a structured conversation around the resilience of the systems we are interested in. The frame was tested in a variety of different situations – from industrial clusters, to cities, to large regions – and with different levels of analysis and data intensity, where it proved itself both useful to spur the right conversations, and to be robust to a variety of contexts and data richness.

Still, the frame is to be seen as primarily as an 'on-ramp' to a richer discussion of resilience. For the sake of simplicity, it leaves out a number of concepts that are important to access a full suite of resilience solutions. In the second part of this chapter we take a guided tour of these additional concepts, aided by the interviews with resilience experts that we carried out as part of our work with the Resilience Action Initiative. These additional concepts, which often take the form of open questions or dilemmas, in part reflect the gulf that still exists between resilience thinking in the abstract, and resilience practice. Still we found them very important and thought provoking, even if sometimes they led to more questions than answers.

A diagnostic frame

We developed a framework with five dimensions that allows a team to capture their current understanding of the resilience issues of a system.

The dimensions consider external stresses to the system, their interrelatedness as well as capabilities for learning and foresight. The framework helps us understand how multiple actions relate to each other, and has been helpful in exploring resilience challenges. It has been tested for a number of different systems through a series of workshops. These 'system elements', represented in the exhibit below, enable, in a simple yet powerful way, a discussion of the most important dimensions of resilience.

The horizontal axis of the framework focuses on the exposure of the system to stresses, inventoried in three categories: resource, societal and acute events stresses. Two additional elements, represented on the vertical axis, focus on how the system's structure affects its response to these stresses, looking at, on the one hand, how the tight coupling of its exposure to different stresses can increase the impact of individual stresses, and, on the other hand, how the system is capable of increasing its resilience through foresight, learning and overall adaptive capacity.

A structured approach to resilience assessment focuses on both system exposure to stresses, and its ability to respond to them

System lens   Resilience elements

Holistic assessment

Response dimension

4 - Learning, foresight & self-organization
- Ability of the system to foresee stresses, learn from and adapt to them, and self-organise in the presence of new challenges

Resilience multipliers

6 - Structural resilience
- Redundancy
- Modularity
- Requisite diversity

1 - Resource stress
- Exposure to and robustness against chronic stresses from resources such as energy, water and food
- Resource productivity levers or alternative resource choices can increase resilience

2 - Societal stress
- Social conditions increasing system vulnerability to chronic and acute stress through e.g.
  - Access to resources
  - Distribution of risks

3 - Acute events stress
- Exposure to and robustness against acute stresses from catastrophes or other acute events
- Adaptation levers or other risk mitigation measures can increase resilience

7 - Integrative resilience
- Multi-scalar interactions
- Thresholds
- Social capital

Exposure dimensions

5 - Interdependency
- System-level correlation and critical dependencies between resources and other stresses (e.g., energy-intensive water sources)

Risk and stress multipliers

8 - Transformative resilience
- Distributed governance
- Foresight capacity
- Innovation and experimentation

We now look in more detail at the three core resilience stresses described on the horizontal axis: (1) Resource stress, (2) Societal stress and (3) Acute events stress.

1. **Resource stress** relates to the exposure of the system to stresses on the energy-water-food nexus, but also its robustness against these stresses. Examples include increasing water scarcity or the depleting fossil reserves. Typical resilience actions include the increase of resource productivity (efficiency increase), the increase of buffers and diversity (efficiency reduction), the replacement of resources, or the reduction of volatility in resource consumption. In examining this dimension of a system's exposure to stress, we found it useful to look at:

   a. **Demand-supply dynamics of the critical resources (e.g. water, energy, food, land).** This can be done qualitatively, but also quantitatively, building a perspective on the demand and supply growth of each resource under different scenarios, and examining what needs to happen to keep supply and demand balanced.

   b. **Supply quality.** It is not enough to examine whether future resources demand can be met – it is important to ask whether it can be done sustainably, what kind of impact future supply sources have on the systems' natural capital, or whether future demand can be met through high dependency on imports, or by a system with limited or no diversification, and with reliability or redundancy challenges.

    c. We finally found it interesting to look at the **resource productivity of the system**: how resource efficient it is today, what improvements on resource stresses can be achieved by improving resource efficiency, e.g. through measures like recycling, and how far the system is from the efficiency versus resilience trade-off when resources are considered.

2. The dimension on **societal stress** relates to the social conditions that increase system vulnerability to chronic and acute event stress. Societal stress should not be limited to the social context of the two other stresses, but should consider social dynamics in a broad sense. The narrow definition includes stress through access to resources, distribution of risk (e.g. unplanned settlement of flood-prone area that increases the exposure to flood risk) or emergent risks (e.g. high level of urban unemployment that increases the impact of food price fly-up on social order or extreme income inequality). Resilience actions include limiting unequal distribution of risk, increasing fairness in resource distribution or social planning

3. The **acute event stress** dimension deals with the exposure of the system to sudden stresses that may jeopardise or severely test its dynamics. Typical examples are natural hazards such as cyclones, floods or droughts, but also sudden price spikes that make a resource economically nearly unavailable. Not all acute stresses are readily identifiable and some of the most powerful are endogenous risks such as the 2008 banking crisis or the Arab Spring. Resilience actions include measures to avoid such stress situations, to increase the absorption capacity, the speed of recovery and the ability to respond to stress. For a number of acute events, it is possible to take a risk management approach at first, to:

    a. Enumerate the principal **hazards** the system is exposed to – from natural catastrophes to extreme price fly-ups on critical traded commodities, understanding their **magnitude and past frequency**. Scientists are finding that certain changes in the statistical patterns may be early indicators of acute events.[4]

    b. Develop a qualitative or quantitative risk perspective, by examining both the **exposure** and the **vulnerability** of the systems to these events, and the **mitigation** actions either in place or possible. A pragmatic quantitative approach to do so with climate risk, for example, has been developed by the Economics of Climate Adaptation group.[5] Beware of implicit assumptions whether the relevant risks follow a *normal* distribution.

---

4   Scheffer (2009).
5   Economics of Climate Adaptation Working Group (2009)

c. Finally it is helpful to think of the **physical and financial recovery mechanisms** the system has already in place, in the form of emergency preparedness and response plans, emergency response procedures, strategic reserves, etc.

The horizontal axis is helpful in guiding a discussion of the system stress in isolation, but the resilience of the system will be tested more severely where stresses are tightly coupled, as represented on the vertical axis.

4. The dimension on **interdependency** takes into consideration system-level correlation and critical dependencies between resources and other stresses – e.g. the energy intensity of water resources and the water intensity of the energy system. This consideration is at the core of the 'stress nexus' concept, where cross-resource intensity accelerates the impact of single resource stresses on the system. In making these considerations it is important to be explicit also about the time scale of cross-resource demand – for example, whether cross-resource intensity tends to concentrate demand peaks, like a hydroelectric system feeding irrigation pumps, all relying on the same water; and also be explicit in considering any critical dependencies in the system that might create important cross-resource thresholds.

5. Finally, we found it extremely helpful to explicitly consider those elements of the system that increase its resilience by providing capacity for **learning, foresight, and self-organisation**. Because resilience is essentially about adaptive capacity, these dimensions provide a good approach to discussing how the system can adapt to foreseen and unforeseen challenges – what **institutions and processes** are in place to **allow for foresight**, e.g. through monitoring of important leading indicators; what is its ability to **capture, store, and share lessons learned and best practices**; and what processes and opportunities are in place for **self-evaluation and change**.

Especially in discussing this last element, we found it useful to think about three different levels or 'elements of resilience', as a parallel lens to use in diagnostic exercises: (6) structural resilience, (7) integrative resilience and (8) transformative resilience.

These lenses[6] are treated in more detail in Chapter 5, but suffice it to introduce them here:

---

6   The choice of these lenses owes a great debt to Walker and Salt (2006) and Walker and Salt (2012).

6. **Structural resilience** focuses on the structural elements building resilience of the system itself, with a view to improve system performance continuity: This includes *redundancy* or putting buffers or spares in the system, *modularity* to separate components and avoid a cascade of failures and *requisite diversity* in those dimensions that are relevant for this particular system at this particular time.

7. **Integrative resilience** emphasises the complex interconnections of the company with its environment. This includes *multi-scale interaction* as described above by mapping the feedback loops between scales, *thresholds* or discontinuities at which point the system goes through a step change and *social capital* describing the accumulated capacity for bottom-up self organization of a society to respond to stress.

8. **Transformative resilience** adds a longer time scale and thus opens the range even more, to ensure and enhance a company's transformability. This includes *distributed governance* in order to tap into the self-organising capacity beyond straightforward top-down interventions, the *foresight capacity* to have a process to include irreducible uncertainties into the envisaged solutions, as well as *innovation and experimentation* as enablers through learning-by-doing.

Throughout the experience of the Resilience Action Initiative, we have used these lenses in a number of workshops to assemble perspectives on the resilience challenges that a system was facing, and to elicit potential interventions. We used them in situations as diverse as the development of new extractive resources in a water-constrained region, the challenges faced by a major industrial port city as it expands its industrial footprint, the resource efficiency challenges of an industrial cluster, and the resilience implication of the energy futures of a middle-income country. Not only did the frame prove itself to be helpful and robust to a different set of resilience challenges, but it also proved itself useful both in situations where the discussion was carried out with little or no prior analysis, which was then guided by the frame, as well as in applications where the frame was used to organise an extensive body of quantitative analysis.

Beyond a diagnostic frame

A framing tool cannot capture all the dimensions of resilience – and we found it doesn't need to. It functions as an on-ramp to make visible the dynamics of the system under consideration, which can then be deepened further through a facilitated discussion in order to determine an action plan. There are a few aspects that featured in those discussions, which are worth highlighting: the consequence of picking system boundaries, how efficiency and resilience relate, the importance of considering multiple scales and making system assumptions explicit and finally some open questions and dilemmas.

The boundary conundrum

In practical terms, analysing a system's resilience requires picking a boundary. Which boundary we choose has specific consequences as it may exclude important influences from outside the boundary. We must be attentive to interactions across the boundary – in particular for fat-tail events that may come from outside the system. In practice, keeping the boundary somewhat fuzzy helps to avoid missing critical interconnections. While this seems like an ambiguous recommendation, it is an inevitable consequence of taking a systemic view: considering too big a system is simply impractical and setting the boundaries too narrowly means we will exclude critical influences.

The difficult relationship between efficiency and resilience

Most people will consider higher efficiency as an absolute good: more efficient is always better than less efficient. As a consequence, the insight that sometimes efficiency comes at the expense of resilience is often both a surprise and a difficult idea to grasp. While the benefits of increasing efficiency are undeniable, the cost of these measures to resilience is rarely assessed. The prize, of course, is having both.

When the tsunami hit Japan in March 2011, it showed that the confidence placed in the sea defenses protecting the Fukushima nuclear power plant was misplaced. The ensuing disruption of the highly efficient just-in-time supply chains for automobile production was massive. Just-in-time production is the ultimate efficiency consideration, where buffers in the chain have been absolutely minimised through a tight coupling of IT systems between factory and suppliers. Windshield wipers are delivered in just the right quantities at just the right time to build them into the cars. The tsunami and accompanying earthquakes thoroughly disrupted this brittle supply chain and it took many months to return to full production. The just-in-time supply chain was an example of efficiency at the expense of resilience. We're not saying what the right trade-off is; a couple of months of lost production, compared to decades of lean manufacturing might well have been the right balance. The point is that in the efficiency frame, this trade-off was not explicitly part of the analysis; in the resilience frame it would be.[7]

This trade-off is linked to the choice of system boundary highlighted above: e.g. the natural world as a whole is efficient, but when you increase the efficiency of an isolated component (e.g. intensive farming), it impacts the resilience of the whole. Most of the time this erosion occurs through the reduction of diversity or the elimination of system buffers.

Weighing resilience and efficiency is hard as efficiency is mostly above dispute. Are buffers really redundant or are you starting to erode the functional diversity that is required for resilience? In other words, to increase efficiency, we reduce the options we have in choosing our responses by making things more homogenous. Much of what is considered redundant tends to be response diversity, i.e. the ability to have multiple strategies to react to something unexpected.

When trading off resilience and efficiency, this issue of the system boundary is essential. Making companies highly efficient may make them individually less resilient, but together they can form a more resilient economy. Similarly, intensive agriculture is necessary to feed humanity – but, in addition, smart efficiency in agriculture can lead to a dramatic reduction in fertiliser and water waste. This contributes to overall resilience by using resources efficiently, in the process of scaling up of food production.

We next turn to the issue of scales.

Dealing with multiple scales

"Managing at a single scale is the single biggest mistake people make in dealing with resilience", states Brian Walker, the head of the Resilience Alliance that connects academics with interest in the topic. With scale we mean, for example, time (short, medium and long term) or space (street, neighborhood, city, country). Inevitably when we consider an issue, we have a focal scale – i.e. the scale at which a solution is intended to be found. This can be a project, an industrial park or a whole ecosystem. Paying heed to the relationships between scales and to the influence that may come from other scales requires explicit focus.

Identifying feedback loops between scales is essential, and can be done by starting the examination with a focal scale, and going up and down a level to map the main feedback loops. In practice, the number of main loops will be

---

7   The example is quoted from Colander and Kupers (2014).

limited, typically around five ('the rule of hand'). The reason is that a system with too many feedback loops would become unstable and rearrange itself with fewer dominant feedback loops. Unfortunately, knowing the right set of feedback loops is not always easy, or even possible. This is an essential difference from considering only feedback at a single system level. Often only feedback loops at the largest scale are considered,[8] such as interaction between the food production in a region with the available water. Yet individual fields and wells may well have an influence at the macro scale. (In the next chapter, water management in the Subak agricultural region is described, which illustrates this point.)

The effect of connections between scales can be to create stress or instabilities that arise seemingly out of thin air. These types of endogenous (emergent) stresses come about through the multi-scalar dynamics. In the 2008 global financial crisis, much weight is put on the sub-prime mortgages as the 'cause' of the crisis. Yet the financial system has weathered much worse 'causes' without such widespread consequences. Looking through a resilience lens would yield a different narrative, one whereby the feedback loops between the different banks, financial networks and regulatory frameworks led to an endogenous shock, plausibly triggered by the sub-prime mortgages.

A multi-scalar perspective is at the heart of resilience – and is much overlooked. It is well known from the science of complex (i.e. interconnected) systems that feedback loops between various scales in a system are the essence of various kinds of emergent behaviours and properties.

Making system assumptions explicit

A widely held, but often hidden assumption, in dealing with socioeconomic issues is to postulate a closed system with a single equilibrium. In such a system a viable solution can be identified, which will be optimal over time. This assumption underlies much of standard macroeconomics and has spread widely as a thought pattern. A system with a single equilibrium has no resilience issues. In such a system, prices drive behaviour, and balances supply and demand. Modern insights in economics and system theory suggest that economies in fact have multiple equilibria. The resilience lens requires making explicit and challenging the assumptions: Is the system open or closed? Does it have a single or multiple optimal equilibria? Do we have a way of selecting an equilibrium?

---

8   Under influence of the Systems Dynamic approach popularised since the 1960s (MIT's Jay Forrester, Club of Rome etc.).

Open questions and dilemmas

"Resilience is always, perhaps maddeningly, provisional, and its insistence toward holism, longer-term thinking, and less-than-peak efficiency represent real ... challenges."[9]

While the frame presented above does not exhaustively describe the system, it has helped unearth new solutions and approaches when applied. A level of 'resilience literacy' is helpful to deepen the analysis, but not necessary for impact. In addition there are dilemmas that remain, in part because systems theory has not provided the answers, let alone articulated them in ways that practitioners find useful.

The first dilemma that is often raised is the understandable call for metrics: we strongly recommend resisting this. Resilience is not a parameter to optimise, either maximise or minimise – and it is value neutral. Buzz Holling,[10] the early champion of resilience, has described the resilience cycle through a figure-eight graph that describes the need for resilience to wane occasionally, to allow for change. When a system is stuck in a bad state, resilience must be reduced, to allow the transformation into a new, more adaptive state. But to reach successful transformational change, a very long-term perspective of the system is required. Transformation is not possible without a shared vision of the future to frame the actions in the present and hence it is important to envision system outcomes as separate from company outcomes. Resilience is only a means.

The tension between efficiency and resilience is challenging. Optimising and controlling a part of a system in isolation can result in the decline of the resilience of the broader system. This is a matter of understanding the impact of the choice of boundary, but also in assessing fit-for-purpose diversity and buffers. These will often come at a cost that will need to be justifiable within a resilience frame. How to value resilience in the context of investment constraints and customer requirements is a key challenge that remains unresolved.

This also raises the question of who is accountable for resilience. For example, in the run up to the financial crisis of 2008, the optimisation of the health of individual banks appears to have eroded the resilience of the overall financial system. In a resilience frame, should banks have been more concerned with the stability of the system? How does resilience affect the

9   Zolli and Healy (2012)
10   Gunderson and Holling (2001)

reach of corporate responsibility? What new types of collaborations are required to achieve resilience?

Solutions to resilience will be found in practical action and will likely not come in the form of blueprints, but in frames that are evolving and adapting. This shifting nature will create tension with the trend towards standardisation and reproduction that is at the heart of the scaling of industrial enterprise, but it opens the opportunity to discover solutions that deliver greater and more long-term value.

3   A resilience lens for enterprise risk management[1]

David N. Bresch,[2] Jaap Berghuijs,[3] Rainer Egloff[4] and Roland Kupers[5]

Enriching corporate risk management

What happens when a fire strikes at the manufacturing plant of the sole supplier of semiconductors used in millions of cell phones? What can a food company do when the natural environment from which it draws its resources is increasingly degraded? And how can a company increase its fitness with respect to unforeseeable challenges? To survive and thrive in the face of stress and disruption, a company can seek for **enterprise resilience**, which we here define as *the capacity of business to survive, successfully adapt and prosper in the face of change and uncertainty related to disturbances with a high impact and a low probability.*

Natural disasters, economic crises, political turmoil, terrorist attacks, environmental degradation and disruptive technologies are just a few examples of the **many kinds of stresses and disruptions** that can impact a company's bottom line. In a global, interconnected world such shocks become more complex, have increasingly big consequences and leave less time to react. Seemingly harmless events, which arrive with little or no perceived warning, may turn out to have serious consequences. It is sometimes only in hindsight that the root causes become visible.

Striving for resilience requires a systemic approach – a strategic and operational perspective that treats the company as a system, and emphasises criteria applicable to any system. A resilience lens in enterprise risk management empowers a company's structural *ability to 'bounce back'* after

---

1   The authors would like to thank the RAI Working Group for its contributions and support, and expresses its gratitude to the participating companies and their risk management representatives for the willingness to share their thoughts and feedback on project drafts in bilateral telephone interviews: Dow, DuPont, IBM, McKinsey & Company, Shell, Siemens and Unilever.
2   Global Head Sustainability, Swiss Re.
3   Junior Strategy Analyst, Reinsurance Strategy, Swiss Re.
4   Senior Risk Manager in Swiss Re's Emerging Risk Management unit.
5   Associate Fellow, Smith School of Enterprise and the Environment, University of Oxford.

a shock or disturbance. It also strengthens the firm's capacity to survive, continuously develop and transform to prosper in complex environments. It prominently does so through *widening the system's horizon*, including social, environmental, economic and emergent factors that a company may not 'own' and be unable to directly control. Finally, to foster the resilience of a company also means to build its *long-term adaptive capacity*. In short, a resilient company can absorb disruption, acknowledge its interconnectedness and proactively change.

Company boards recognise that both the speed with which risk events unfold and their impact on business appears to escalate. They express concerns that their current risk practice no longer adequately protects their company.[6] 'Black swans'[7] or 'fat tails' have been recognised for some time now, yet much of risk management still heavily relies on traditional *Value at Risk* (VaR) analysis assuming normal risk distributions and to a large extent neglects uncertainty, i.e. risks with hard-to-define probability. A company that **ignores fat tails** underestimates its total risk exposure. On the other hand, the effective anticipation of rare high-impact disruption can lead to a competitive advantage, and thus should be viewed as a business opportunity.

Traditional enterprise risk management is optimised to assess and mitigate risks that follow normal statistical distributions, i.e. that are well defined, linear and measurable. However, it does not account well for risks that are difficult to model because of their non-linearity, multidimensionality, propagation over multiple scales or by their mere rareness to actualise. A resilience perspective in enterprise risk management shares many traits with traditional Enterprise Risk Management (ERM) – it supports the survival and thriving of business. It enhances a more traditional focus by applying a systemic approach and by emphasising low probability, slowly accumulating, discrete or unknown risk, dynamic developments, feedback loops and thresholds. The main goal of enterprise resilience is to ensure the adaptability of a company – subjected to an acute or chronic stress, and with a long-term perspective.

We propose a set of resilience lenses grouped in three dimensions or levels: **Structural resilience** focuses on the systemic nature of the company itself, with a view to improve business continuity management. *Redundancy, modularity* and *requisite diversity* are important aspects to this. **Integrative resilience** emphasises the complex interconnections of the company

---

6   PwC (2011), 3
7   Taleb (2007)

with its environment. We highlight *multi-scale interaction*, *thresholds* and *social capital*. Finally, **transformative resilience** adds a longer time scale and so opens the range even more, to ensure and enhance a company's transformability. Here we discuss *distributed governance*, *foresight capacity*, and *innovation and experimentation* as enablers. One can also frame the presented lenses as different facets of the same prism providing different ways to look at the same thing: the resilience dynamics of an enterprise. The structuring in levels – from structural to transformative – allows shifting focal scale: from (1) the company through (2) its interconnections with its environments to (3) long-term adaptability.

The project documented here is part of the Resilience Action Initiative (RAI). Privately launched at WEF 2012, RAI was set up with the vision of business, by working and innovating together, making their value chains and local economic partners (i.e. at city and regional level) more resilient to stresses arising from the energy-water-food nexus, amplified by climate change risk factors. This chapter turns the focus of resilience to the companies themselves, going beyond a mere focus on the energy-water-food nexus. The chapter represents a pioneering effort, stressing the importance of putting resilience on the enterprise risk management map. For the individual company, this chapter serves as a starting point to deal with resilience, from which its resilience approach can be 'customised' according to the specific environment and factors of importance for that company. Because specific resilience requirements may vary strongly between industries and companies, we here deliberately refrain from providing detailed practical advice on an individual company basis.

Similar type of disaster – different effects: Deepwater Horizon vs Exxon Valdez

The comparison of two equivalent high-impact low-probability events, the 1989 Exxon Valdez and 2010 Deepwater Horizon oil spills, illustrates how the risk landscape has changed in recent times. Both spills were the largest ever in American waters at their time, had a severe environmental impact and resulted in the pollution of vast stretches of US coastline. From an enterprise risk perspective, however, a strong contrast between the two disasters exists.

While the Exxon Valdez spill resulted in strong uproar amongst locals and environmentalists, other stakeholders largely ignored the incident. This gave Exxon ample time, first to handle clean-up operations and subsequently to take a strictly legalistic hard line on claims and regulatory issues. News of the Deepwater Horizon catastrophe, on the other hand, instantly spread around the world and produced an outcry from stakeholders and the general public through digital social media that did not yet exist 20 years before. Extensive media coverage, including 24-hour webcam footage of oil spewing from the well, made the world's eyes turn to the incident and lead to close scrutiny of BP's reaction to the event.

In contrast to Exxon's 1989 spill, in 2010 BP only had a fraction of the time of its predecessor to react while the impact of the event was much more severe, both regarding environmental damage and from an enterprise risk point of view. The enterprise-wide reputational damage for BP was enormous, and the event's impacts have swept across the industry.

Source: Adapted from PwC (2011)

Structural resilience

The focus of structural resilience, which is also known as 'engineering resilience', lies on *bouncing back faster after stress, enduring greater stresses, and being disturbed less by a given amount of stress.*[8] In other words, this first level of resilience is all about enhancing capacity to withstand disruption. It concentrates on resilience aspects that are internal to a given company, such as its strategy and organisational structure. Structural resilience aspects and measures are therefore easiest to implement and control, and form a fundamental step to increase resistance against disruption. Structural resilience comprises three different lenses – redundancy, modularity and requisite diversity – each of which will be discussed below.

Redundancy
Before September 11, 2001, many financial service firms had a massive network of IT infrastructure in and around the World Trade Center, which formed an important connection to the US markets. When the terrorist attack on and subsequent collapse of the towers left Deutsche Bank's New York's facility in ruins, redundant IT systems in Ireland took over operations. On the very same day, the company was able to clear more than USD300 billion with the Fed.[9] Deutsche Bank used a conceptually simple and intuitive way of limiting the potential impact of disruption: the introduction of redundancy, i.e. putting in place **buffers** that can absorb the impact of

8   *Martin-Breen and Anderies (2011)*
9   Sheffi (2007)

a shock. Such buffers can be of many different kinds and generally come at a cost, such as the safety stock kept by a manufacturing company or redundant production capacity for a company's most important product lines. Redundancy also comes with company size: a large multinational has more physical and financial capital to absorb shocks of a given size than a medium-sized enterprise. It provides overcapacity that protects against critical failure or, more plainly put, keeps the company running when it receives a blow.

While redundancy is a simple and effective measure to increase resilience, it goes against the efficiency push many companies established over the last decades. Cutting inventories and building leaner supply chains resulted in a very high efficiency and a strong increase in quality of products and services. Rather than reversing the gains of these efforts, companies need to critically assess the **costs and benefits of redundancy** in its different forms and independently determine their own position in the trade-off between resilience and efficiency.

Modularity

In businesses that are internally strongly connected, shocks that initially only hit a small part of the company may propagate rapidly, causing extensive damage. Conversely, in an organisation with a modular internal structure, such **shocks can be contained**, and business is more easily restored. Modularity can be understood as a form of decentralisation, which has several additional advantages. Decentralised decision-making, such as in many franchises, empowers those who know the local business environment best. This ensures faster as well as more accurate and effective action than in a centrally governed organisation. Also, decentralised supply chains focusing on local suppliers are less vulnerable to shocks.

Another benefit of modularity is the **exchangeability of individual components**, which allows for dynamic reorganisation and more flexibility. Systems may appear complex from the outside but often have a surprisingly simple, modular internal structure consisting of components that plug into one another – much like Lego blocks – and, equally importantly, can be unplugged and reconfigured easily when necessary.[10] This allows for a much faster and more dynamic reaction to changing circumstances.

Additionally, a modular structure allows for **scaling up and scaling down** – the ability to flock or swarm – by increasing or decreasing the number of linkages between components or by breaking them, whichever

10   Zolli and Healy (2012)

a specific situation might call for. This ability to flock or swarm increases a company's adaptive capacity – the ability to aptly react to a situational change. Cloud computing, for which linked, redundant servers are used to complete a specific task, forms a specific example.

A modular organisational structure, however, does have certain **disadvantages**. Increased independency of organisational modules can result in a loss of uniformity, which can cause problems with safety and risk tolerance. These disadvantages can be offset with a global governance framework based on principles, standards and a strong company culture. However, one should be aware of the danger in translating such global principles into local rules, as this can effectively annul the intended modularity. Introducing less visible links can make the modules act in concert. The 2008 financial crisis made it apparent that investment resilience through portfolio diversification often failed, as other financial instruments had forged strong de facto connections between portfolio elements. Similarly, if companies adopt modularity as a resilience strategy, they should critically inspect the implicit interdependencies between the modules. On a USD70 trillion global annual economy, the $600 billion bankruptcy filing of Lehman Brothers in mid-September 2008 was a relatively modest event. However, through an epidemic of fear and uncertainty it lead to a global collapse of the financial system. The crisis revealed that the system of financial companies and institutions, although modular, was (and remains) vulnerable because it was much more strongly connected than it was previously perceived.

Requisite diversity

Diversity is most often discussed and applied in the human resources. Workforce diversity often refers to the gender ratio in a company or in its upper management, to the ethnical background or age of employees, to the representation of cultural and language groups, etc. Such aspects of workforce diversity all contribute to diversity of thought and skills, which stimulates discussion, fosters wiser and more considered decisions, and enhances creativity and innovation. In other words, they enhance **functional diversity** and allow a company to operate more effectively.

More important in the context of enterprise resilience, however, is what is commonly referred to as **responsive diversity**[11]: Various 'components' (i.e. employees, systems, strategies, suppliers, production methods, services, etc.) within a functional group respond dissimilarly to different kinds of disturbances. This is most valuable when disaster strikes. For example, a

11   Walker and Salt (2006)

diversified supply chain enables a company to cope much better with any particular disruption within that chain; a diverse set of strategies allows an enterprise to react more effectively to a change in market conditions. Analogously to a portfolio of financial products and irrespective of whether disruption is anticipated, a company with a whole range of diversified components is less prone to company-wide shocks because its risk is spread through responsive diversity.

Diversity may be associated with reduced short-term efficiency. Inhomogeneous subsystems (whether that is a workforce, supply chain, strategy or product portfolio) can demand more time and effort to manage because with diversity, certain advantages of economies of scale are lost. Diversity should not go unchallenged, and companies will be wise to ask what the appropriate focus and amount for diversity may be in particular circumstances. To increase its resilience, a company should constantly determine the right amount of diversity in all relevant components; it should strive for **requisite diversity**.

South Korean electronics giant Samsung believes it can leverage on its diversity range of products and strategies. While it is challenging to be successful in many businesses at the same time, it gives the company an advantage over its more specialised competitors in several ways. For example, Samsung adjusts more easily to the common trend of blurring lines between product segments – as, for example, is the case for mobile phones and tablets. Further, a diverse range of relatively similar products, combined with a high reaction speed to the market's response, allows the company to discover and cater for new markets quickly. The successful combination of diversity and agility proves useful both to seize opportunity and to adjust to shocks – it adds to the company's adaptive capacity and, therefore, to its resilience.[12]

Structural resilience: Rabobank's unique organisation

Rabobank ranks amongst the top-20 banks in the world by equity and is one of the few that remained relatively unscathed during the 2008 financial crisis. Unlike many others, it did not require government support. Can we pinpoint the origin of its higher resilience?

Its origins in 1890 as a cooperative agricultural micro-finance bank endowed it a unique cooperative structure. Today, it is a network of 140 member banks,

12   Nisen (2013)

which in turn have thousands of individual members. But the recognition of its importance waxed and waned, with a full-fledged effort to convert it into a conventional structure with a stock market listing in the 1990s ultimately resulting in a recommitment to the membership structure in 1998. Its strongest binding factor is the cross-guarantee, under which any individual Rabobank guarantees the obligations of all other member banks. The power balance within the Rabobank Group is a delicate equilibrium between the local banks on the one hand and the central organisation on the other. Although Rabobank lost its rare AAA credit in 2012, its unique structure is seen as a key resource for managing uncertainty in turbulent times and it has been ranked amongst the ten safest banks in the world.

In general cooperative banks with their distributed governance structures have had superior performance during the financial crisis. There are a number of explanations for their higher resilience, in which the corporate governance structure plays an important role in dealing with systemic risks. Member ownership entails a conservative banking approach with a longer-term perspective and a focus on retail banking. Cooperative banks are characterised by relatively lower risks, lower volatility and more stable returns. CEO Smits writes: "It is the task of the top-management to manage these multiple hierarchies and to keep them in a future-proof balance."

Source: Adapted from Boonstra (2010) and Van Dijk (1999)

Integrative resilience

Any enterprise is embedded in a complex natural-social-economic system, which is constituted and influenced by many different factors and stakeholders – such as competitors, the financial markets, the natural environment and the general public. Many firms, in turn, possess the ability to influence this overall system. A company and its surrounding system are interconnected in many different, often poorly understood ways. Integrative resilience therefore requires an opening of focus from the individual company to the larger system it is embedded in or linked to. In order to become more resilient, a company needs to acknowledge this mutual dependency, and to understand its inherent risks and opportunities. *Multi-scale interaction*, *thresholds* and *social capital* are eminent concerns of *integrative resilience*.

Multi-scale interaction
Consider the 2007 '**tortilla riots**' in Mexico – a series of public protests against the strong price rises of corn, the main ingredient of tortillas. The

corn price spike resulted from a strong dependence on American corn suppliers, which were able to sell their excess corn below production cost due to NAFTA. In the USA, corn prices went up as production was switched to fuel ethanol in many places, in response to a disruption in oil production in the Gulf of Mexico because of Hurricane Katrina, which hit the area in 2005. This example shows that seemingly disconnected events, such as a rise in food prices, result from the complex interaction between multiple system scales, which include financial, political, social and environmental aspects that each move at different speeds.[13]

Systems thinking[14] acknowledges that a natural-social-economic system consists of many different scales. It is the **interaction between different scales** that drives the emergent behaviour of the system in which a company is embedded. Changes on one of these scales influence the processes in others, which is why it is unhelpful to treat any of these scales or processes in isolation. All too often, decisions are made without understanding their broader, long-term and systemic impact. A simple way to look at this is to establish the **focal scale**, take a step up and a step down in scale, and map the interactions.

Any publicly listed company faces the time-scale related conflict of ensuring sustainable, long-term company success with delivering immediate results to shareholders. Conflicts and trade-offs between short- and long-term targets naturally affect the quest for resilience itself. Many of the resilience aspects discussed here reduce rather than improve a company's short-term efficiency, yet prove very beneficial in the long run. A difficult but necessary step towards resilience is the **focus on diverse time scales** for success.

In 2002 Anglo American, one of the world's largest diversified mining companies, introduced a comprehensive AIDS prevention programme in the workplace that addressed the problem on multiple levels. On an individual employee basis, the company offered voluntary counselling and HIV testing. Awareness, education and prevention campaigns were run and AIDS drugs made available for the whole workforce as well as all their dependents. Addressing the issue on a wider community level initially was a huge financial leap of faith, but it paid off – the efforts had a very positive economic impact and enabled Anglo's business to thrive and grow.[15]

13   Zolli and Healy (2012)
14   Attempts to formulate a transdisciplinary General System Theory go back to the interwar period. Since the 1960's systems thinking became a recognised paradigm to integrate both natural and social sciences, but also other fields like engineering, Systems thinking defines unifying principles, valid for all systems across fields. See von Bertalanffy (1968) or Senge (1990).
15   Voice of America (2010)

Thresholds

Any system has boundaries. Once these are crossed, the system functions in fundamentally different ways. Although such system boundaries or thresholds can be approached both very slowly (e.g. climate change or fundamental shifts in consumer tastes) or very rapidly (2008 financial crisis), when the threshold is reached, change within the system occurs very rapidly in either case. Crucially, many thresholds can only be crossed in one direction – there is often no way back. In order to be resilient, a company must therefore identify its systemic position and trajectory, increase its **own capacity to adapt**, but it may as well strive to **strengthen the surrounding system's resistance** against undesirable change.

A nautical chart does not help much navigating the ocean without any tools for determining a ship's location. Similarly, for a company it is only of limited use to identify critical thresholds of its natural-social-economic environment without knowing where it is with respect to those thresholds. It is therefore essential that relevant, regular and reliable – in other words, appropriate – **feedback loops** (with appropriate sensors) are in place, through which essential information arrives and can be interpreted by the organisation.

Often, a company alone cannot influence the system sufficiently to prevent it from adverse change (e.g. prevent climate change from happening) and in that sense does not have a real choice. In order to survive, adaptation is the only option. As a first step however, it is important to **be aware** of the system's drivers and their respective thresholds. Effective adaptation and risk mitigation need time, which is why early detection, best-possible understanding and effective communication of risks are essential.

After decades of optimisation, farmers in the Goulburn-Broken Catchment in Australia have become some of the world's most efficient in producing high-quality, low-priced milk in large quantities. However, most of the dairying depends on the irrigation of pasture, which also flushes salt down that gets left behind as pastures take up water. While a decrease in irrigation would result in salt accumulation towards the top two metres of soil, an increase would result in a groundwater level rise that brings the salt up as well – which is currently only stopped by pumping. Clearly, the system is on a tight balance between two thresholds, and can only continue to function as long as no major shock occurs.[16]

16   Walter et al. (2009).

Social capital

The importance of social capital reaches further than merely avoiding social unrest by being a good neighbour.[17] Maintaining a good relationship with all stakeholders – not just with local residents but also with governments, customers and suppliers – is essential to a company's business,[18] whether to support its licence to operate, or to keep the local customer base satisfied. In the age of social media, local social problems can turn into global reputation risks at a speed that was unimaginable even ten years ago. However, most companies today also recognise that the potential benefits of investing in a good relationship with external stakeholders reach **beyond downside risk mitigation.** Customer advice and ideas help to improve products; environmental and safety issues may be discovered and reported by attentive local residents. Active collaboration with customers, suppliers and local communities can provide a great amount of added value, which is why the investment in social capital should also be considered an opportunity.

In a resilience context, it is important to realise that many external risks just cannot be mitigated by a company in isolation, but requires a reservoir of good will and the cooperation of multiple stakeholders across corporate boundaries. For example, a company can closely cooperate with its suppliers in response to supply chain disruptions, as the intense cooperation between Philips and Nokia after a disruptive fire in a production plant has proven. A recent study looking at climate impact to the US Gulf Coast calls for concerted action by the private sector, government and general public to fight the consequences of climate change.[19] The prior establishment of trust and strong networks – building bridges between stakeholders – are essential factors to enable such effective cooperation that is necessary for **risk mitigation at a systemic level.**

Coca-Cola has dedicated itself to global water neutrality, is tackling its packaging, recycling and global carbon footprint and tries to help its communities wherever they are – not merely to fend off public scrutiny but, as CEO Muhtar Kent put it, because "the beauty of [such efforts] is that they're actually very good for business, too".[20] Clean, accessible water obviously is essential for Coca-Cola's beverage production but also connects the company to local ecosystems and the health and economic prosperity of communities that host the bottling plants. Coca-Cola recognises that these same com-

17   Turnbull et al. (2013)
18   Starr et al. (2003)
19   Entergy et al. (2010)
20   Ignatius (2011)

munities also form its consumer base. It sells its products where they are made, which means that if communities stay strong, business stays strong.

Transformative resilience

Abruptly changing market conditions, climate change-induced environmental conditions or disruptive social and cultural developments – companies become subject to sudden, drastic changes in operating circumstances. If a company does not anticipate and proactively respond to changes in the system it is embedded in, it will risk going out of business. To adapt to both abrupt and slow but critical changes therefore is the key to the ultimate level of enterprise resilience. We here refer to the ability of an enterprise to reorganise, restructure, and even reinvent when appropriate, both in response to and in anticipation of system changes, as transformative resilience. Evaluation of *governance models*, *foresight capacity* as well as *innovation and experimentation* each support in a specific way the proactive adaptation embodied in *transformative resilience*.

Governance models
According to its size, principal line of business, internal differentiation etc., a company may evaluate different models of governance – conventional and unconventional ones. *Distributed governance* e.g. implies management that is undertaken from multiple centres of authority at different levels, rather than from a single decision-making unit. This concept is also known as 'polycentric governance',[21] which is well known in the public sector – for example, in the context of irrigation systems and forest management. Compared to classic, hierarchical governance, distributed decision-making can lead to better results for complex and ambiguous tasks: for simple linear tasks, top-down control is often most effective, particularly in the short term. In distributed governance, within clearly defined boundaries of authority, decisions can be made independently, immediately and can be implemented at their most effective level. The agility and flexibility of such a governance system as a whole allows it to cope very effectively with a diverse range of risk events, to adapt itself to change and even to evolve over time, in line with new problems that arise. In a continuously changing risk landscape, this capacity to **dynamically reorganise**[22] is crucial in securing long-term resilience.

---

21   Ostrom (2010)
22   Zolli and Healy (2009)

Distributed governance works if effective interconnections and alignments exist between the interest and behaviour of individual stakeholders and that of a system as a whole – and consequently for all stakeholders. A simple example can be drawn from resource management. Sustainable water usage in water-scarce regions requires the cooperation of all stakeholders from both within and outside the company. While it may be in the short-term interest of any individual stakeholder to use more than its fair share of water, in the long term, such behaviour will deplete the resource and cause the system to collapse. Multiple governing authorities at different scales enable holistic management of such issues, whether environmental, economic or social, but require trust and effective communication between all stakeholders and decision-makers. An example for such multi-stakeholder partnership is the Cities for Climate Protection (CCP) programme, a transnational municipal network aimed at reducing urban greenhouse gas emissions that involves both state and non-state actors. The programme operates globally but is governed on national, regional and municipal levels that simultaneously address climate change issues on different scales.[23]

It is important to acknowledge that with governance models, one size does not fit all. Just as this is the case for other aspects of resilience, the fact that **every organisation is different** means that there is no single most effective governance system. Companies themselves should be purposeful in their governance and go beyond the simplicity of single point accountability as a panacea. Many different factors should be taken into consideration, such as the type of industry, business, or product of the company as well as the degree of dependency on the system it is embedded in.

Foresight capacity
Foresight refers to a company's effort to actively engage itself with future events that are inherently uncertain and have an unquantifiable probability of occurrence. Foresight is fundamentally different from forecasting – the prediction of the future based on the extrapolation of data from the past. It is not only that there is not enough data to know the future, but many aspects are in fact unknowable. Although an effective foresight strategy can shape itself in different ways, it generally serves two purposes: foresight can **decrease corporate risk exposure** and helps to **identify business opportunities**. Describing multiple plausible futures and understanding

---

23 For more information on the Cities for Climate Protection programme, go to: http://en.wikipedia. org/wiki/Cities_for_Climate_Protection_program#Decentralisation_of_the_CCP_program.

their impacts on present decision-making, allows the company to integrate uncertainty into their planning and actions.

An effective foresight strategy may comprise scenario planning,[24,25] emerging risk detection, modelling, war-gaming[26], visioning, reverse stress testing,[27] red team simulations[28], or any other means of engagement with the future, depending on the specific needs of a company and the character of the economic system it operates in. Irrespective of its exact form, such **foresight activity increases resilience** because it allows a company to adapt to and reduce vulnerability against potential disruptions and their common consequences before these actually occur. As the Shell Scenarios team has famously shown during the 1973 oil crisis[29], even if no specific mitigation measures are taken, mere awareness enables a quicker reaction that can be enough to give the company a crucial edge over its competitors – that is, as long as challenges such as obtaining the sincere interest of upper management and dealing with too high expectations about taming the future are met.

Tackling a security threat, even before it becomes an issue to be dealt with – that is what Singapore's Institute of Policy Studies aims to do with its Prism scenarios. The scenarios present a set of alternative stories of how the country may govern itself over the next ten years based on three driving forces – credibility of government, society's definition of success, and distribution of resources. Rather than a prediction of the future, the scenario-planning method is designed to help question assumptions and develop flexible mental models for operating in the future.[30]

Innovation & experimentation
In 1999, the chairman of home appliance market leader Whirlpool set out to make innovation a core competence at the company. Over a period of three years, the company involved roughly 10,000 employees in the search for innovation breakthroughs. Some 7,000 ideas where created, which spawned 3,000 small-scale experiments and led to a whole stream of new products and businesses. The success of this focus on innovation transformed the company for good. Today, Whirlpool continues to be recognised for its

24   Wilkinson and Kupers (2013)
25   Dunn Cavelty et al. (2011)
26   Starr et al. (2003)
27   PwC (2011)
28   Sheffi (2007)
29   Wilkinson and Kupers (2013)
30   IPS (2012)

innovation. It actively manages a broad pipeline of ideas, experiments, and major projects from across the company.[31]

Any company that wants to survive in an uncertain future has to be ready to react swiftly to a wide range of possible scenarios. A resilient company therefore does not depend on a single product, strategy, technology or supplier but rather aims to create diversity in every aspect of business – analogous to a financial portfolio.[32, 33] Under continuously changing circumstances, whether these comprise an abrupt shock such as a financial crisis or a slow system shift like climate change, previously successful activities of an enterprise may no longer be beneficial. In this regard, innovation and experimentation are crucial as they enable the creation of new ideas and options – they increase diversity in all aspects of the business portfolio. A resilient company has the capability to self-renew over time through innovation – aimed at **invention, not optimisation** – and experimentation, by reinventing business models as strategies and circumstances change.[34]

Long-term resilience: The Subak system of Bali

Examples of successfully harnessing risk for long-term resilience are rare in the corporate world, but we may draw inspiration from the terraced rice field systems in southern Bali known as the Subak. This millenary system manages known risks such as pests and water, but also unknown risks from internal warfare, colonisation, natural disasters, the Green Revolution and, increasingly, tourists.

Traditional Balinese techniques for water control and terrace management are based on principles nearly opposite to those of the top-down control structures favoured by the planners. The Balinese manage things from the bottom-up, by means of nested hierarchies of water temples that cooperate in setting irrigation schedules. These temples are ritual places where farmers make decisions on water flows and construction. Since the whole system is deeply interconnected, both through the spread of pests and water; no decision stands in isolation.

The Subak system has been simulated 'in silico' in order to understand its resilience to changing circumstance. Not only does it perform in the computer as in the rice fields, but more strikingly the simulation shows how governance system itself will co-evolve with the nature of the problems. As such the governance is not only multi-scalar and polycentric, but it is also itself adaptive to

31   Hamel & Välikangas (2003)
32   Välikangas (2004)
33   Zolli and Healy (2012)
34   Reinmoeller & van Baardwijk (2005)

emerging risks. In June 2012, the Subak has been designated a UNESCO cultural landscape world heritage site, throwing a new problem – that of tourist hordes – at the adaptive capacity of the system. UNESCO aims to identify and preserve such cases of resilient resource governance.

The risk management approach of the Subak holds lessons and provides new science-based tools to be adapted in corporate structures for resilience to systemic risks.

Sources: Fox (2012), Lansing (2006), Lansing (1993), Schmuki (2009)

Conclusion

We have introduced a concept of enterprise resilience that builds on three pillars or levels. For each resilience level we described different relevant aspects or **resilience lenses**, and we gave examples of adaptation measures. Note that these measures should be considered as examples only, since their relevance and effectiveness strongly depends on the character of the specific company and the system in which it is embedded. However, this does not take away from the fact that the resilience lenses themselves are relevant for business across industries.

Structural resilience is about internal adaptation measures that a company can adopt to become more resistant to disruption. It includes the assessment of cost and benefits of *redundancy* and determines trade-offs between resilience and efficiency. It identifies adequate *modularity*, such as the decentralising of service and production chains. Shocks reveal whether enough responsive diversity is in place, and they can be dealt with and avoided by cultivating functional or *requisite diversity*.

Integrative resilience acknowledges that companies are embedded in a social-environmental-economic system, with which they need to interact both to cope more effectively with disruption and be more agile when it comes to seizing opportunity. As companies are part of complex *multi-scale interactions,* effective enterprise resilience allows the establishment of an adequate focal scale (including time scales) for each and every problem, and the mapping of linkages 'up/further' and 'down/closer' from or to this scale. It is adopted to identify *critical thresholds* and closely looks into feedback loops, not least to monitor system status with respect to thresholds. Finally, it's crucial to build public trust or *social capital* well in advance of crises, as it will be difficult to impossible to develop these relationships under stress.

Transformative resilience builds on the former lenses, but additionally calls for continuous adaptation and transformation needed to survive and thrive under new operating circumstances. *Distributed governance* allows for sustainably self-organised adaptation. Compared to classic, hierarchical governance, distributed decision-making leads to better results for complex and ambiguous tasks – and allows for emergent response in turbulent times. Resilient enterprise management creates and safeguards a safe space to explore options under various *scenarios. Foresight capacity* increases awareness and alertness that reaches beyond specific mitigation measures. Last but not least, continuous *innovation and experimentation* allow a company to learn faster than its competitors – it increases adaptive capacity.

COMPANIES'
RESILIENCE

4   Multi-sector collaboration for resilience

Mark Smith[1]

Change is a challenge familiar to corporate leaders. Professor John Kotter of Harvard Business School, in his classic book *Leading Change*,[2] set out an 8-step process for successfully managing change in organisations. These build from creating a sense of urgency and convening a coalition of champions through to empowering people to take action and embedding change in new cultures. Kotter argued for strategies for managing change that are not trapped by top-down, command-and-control dominance. He made the case that organisational change will be more successful where efforts are made to help people to re-learn the expectations and norms within an organisation, supported by data, communications, empowerment and learning-by-doing. In the public realm, the language used may be different, but the ingredients for change are similar. Based on the Nobel Prize-winning work of Elinor Ostrom, adaptive governance of natural resources, for example, is more effective in achieving beneficial change where decentralised, self-organising institutions are rich in information and empowered to make decisions on collective action through dialogue and deliberation.[3] Whether the aim is organisational change or adaptive governance, both represent processes of social change put to work to reshape and re-orient a system from within. Both provide some clues on how to tackle the broader challenge of change in complex systems that is needed to build resilience.

Johan Rockström and colleagues laid out an hypothesis in a 2009 paper in the journal *Nature* that the human population, through natural resource exploitation, is pushing against 'planetary boundaries' and losing its 'safe operating space'.[4] This points to a world that is becoming riskier and, as Earth-system thresholds are approached and crossed, more prone to instability and surprise. Thomas Homer-Dixon wrote of five 'tectonic stresses' that link ecological, social and economic pressures and amplify risks:

Energy stress – especially from increasing scarcity of conventional oil,

Economic stress – from more instability in the global economy and a widening gap between rich and poor,

---

1   Director, Global Water Programme, International Union for Conservation of Nature (IUCN).
2   *Kotter* (1996)
3   Dietz, Ostrom and Stern (2003)
4   Rockström et al. (2009)

Demographic stress – from differences in population growth between rich and poor societies and from expansion of megacities,

Environmental stress – from worsening damage to land, water, forests and fisheries, and

Climate stress – from changes in the composition of Earth's atmosphere.[5]

Both natural systems and the global economy are becoming more turbulent under these converging and interconnected stresses. There is, however, a competing narrative, as global GDP is projected to almost double by 2030 (from a 2010 baseline), from $50 to $95 trillion, driving growth in demand for primary energy of 33%, food of 27% and water of 41%.[6] There are contradictions in these narratives. In a riskier, more turbulent world, reconciling them will need transformations that make communities, ecosystems, the economy and societies more resilient. Deep change is needed in the complex dynamics of the social and ecological systems that shape the future.

The private sector, governments and civil society have interests that align with changes needed to build resilience. Each sector needs effective strategies for building resilience that will help them succeed in achieving their goals in a more turbulent world. Just as leaders in each of these sectors need effective strategies for organisational change to ensure that their businesses, agencies or NGOs are dynamic, effective and adaptive, they need tools for creating the changes needed for societies to become more resilient. Just as Kotter understood organisational change as a social process, they will need to find avenues for collaboration, empowerment and learning needed to change complex systems from within.

Change for resilience

Resilience means being able to survive, adapt and improve in the face of stress and change, to be able to withstand shocks, but reorganise and rebuild when necessary. The capacity to bounce back, but 'bounce forward' to a better state if possible. Humanity's response over millennia to new demographic, environmental or climatic stresses, or to energy constraints in the economy or natural resource scarcity, has been invention and innovation. New technologies have repeatedly emerged to deliver not only solutions, but also economic advancement that has created new employment and new

5   Homer-Dixon (2006)
6   Dobbs et al. (2011)

national wealth, new entrepreneurship and new value for companies and their shareholders. In a world of converging stresses where there are Earth-system thresholds and tipping points at play, a different path is needed.

Current technological pathways, while hugely successful historically, have favoured narrow optimisation of solutions to problems. Over time, unintended social and environmental consequences have accumulated – such as climate change, species extinctions, fisheries collapse or impoverishment downstream from hydropower dams. Seen through a systems lens, technological innovation has tended to help in optimising exploitation of individual natural resources, industrial sectors or enterprises, but caused broader 'knock-on' effects across social-ecological systems. These effects are typically poorly understood or unknown because of complexity. In response, investment to improve knowledge of how social and environmental impacts unfold has increased. With the speed of technological advance and global interconnectedness, however, the unknown impacts of actions accumulate faster than knowledge of them. Requirements for innovation are hence accelerating as global stresses converge but knowledge cannot keep pace,[7] creating an 'ingenuity gap' that technology alone cannot bridge.[8] The technological pathways we have relied on historically are not suited, by themselves, to the deeper changes needed to provide the building blocks for resilience to converging stresses.

Collaboration for systemic change

Innovation for resilience must influence the workings of complex systems, with uncertainties, unknowns and nonlinearities at play. It needs to help communities, companies or countries develop leverage they can use to bounce back or bounce forward – to survive, reorganise, learn and improve in a future more prone to instability and surprise. Innovation for resilience contributes to systems change, with social, economic and environmental dimensions. It needs to provoke and steer transformations beyond technological change, of management regimes, governance and the ways natural capital and social capital are built (or rebuilt) alongside economic value.

In a past era, there might have been an expectation that it was the job of governments alone to set such transformations in motion. Today, however, society's toughest problems are increasingly being tackled by collaborations

7   Westley et al. (2011)
8   Homer-Dixon (2000)

that combine the capacities, talents, reach and resources of the public and private sectors and civil society. In *The Solution Revolution*, William Eggers and Paul MacMillan tell the stories of citizens, businesses and philanthropists who are working together to solve problems rather than relying solely on the public sector.[9] Cross-sector collaborations aim to leverage business and social entrepreneurship, social networks and new kinds of investment alongside platforms for negotiating consensus. Multi-sector collaboration is being used by governments, business and civil society to activate change.

Collaboration has in part grown out of the experience of conflicts between communities and companies. Public and NGO pressure in natural resource sectors (energy, mining, forestry, agriculture), for example, has undermined social 'licence to operate', increased costs and, ultimately, forced companies out of particular markets. Companies face costs; therefore, they shrink from societal change. Governments can help by putting in place rules to create sanctions and incentives that encourage companies to invest in change and avoid social conflict. As standards and regulations have tightened, many companies have learned in response that the better path, instead of battling protestors in the courts, markets or even physically, is to work with stakeholders to avoid or mitigate environmental and social impacts of business operations. They work collaboratively with civil society and governments to 'co-create' solutions. Companies have learned, further, that possessing the skills needed for stakeholder engagement and co-creativity brings competitive advantage.[10]

Case 1 – Marine Stewardship Council

The global seafood industry was under intense public and consumer pressure in the 1990s because unsustainable fishing practices were blamed for severe degradation of marine ecosystems. With the collapse of the Newfoundland cod fishery in the early 1990s, there were calls for urgent action to halt the overexploitation of major fisheries around the world, to protect not only the marine environment, but also fishing livelihoods.

Unilever, the largest fish retailer at the time, and the World Wide Fund for Nature (WWF) joined forces to respond. They jointly led and financed a two-year process to build consensus around the design for a sustainability standard for marine fisheries and to launch an organisation to develop and operate a certification scheme. With effective leadership, resistance to a standard from many fishing companies and some governments was overcome, and in 1999 the Marine

9   Eggers and MacMillan (2013)
10 Higginson and Vredenburg (2010)

Stewardship Council (MSC) was launched as an independent organisation. Almost 15 years later, 10% of global marine fish harvest is certified through MSC, with a value of $3 billion annually. The MSC operates as a non-profit, under governance that brings together civil society and business, including through a Stakeholder Advisory Council comprising representatives from NGOs, academia, fishing companies and trawling industry associations. The MSC is contributing to pulling many fisheries back from the threat of collapse, or at least slowing the approach.

In the case of innovation for resilience, governments, civil society and the private sector have different motivations but they share interests in a more resilient future. Governments aim, for example, to find resilient pathways to creating prosperity in a riskier world. Civil society aims to use its networks and knowledge to champion solutions for resilience based on social justice or a reawakening to benefits from nature conservation. For business, resilience will help to build and protect long-term shareholder value under converging stresses, but transitions to resilience also offer opportunities, as customers will increasingly need expertise and services that strengthen resilience. Understanding among sectors of mutual advantage and opportunities in supporting greater public good through resilience will be key.[8]

Case 2 – Urban Resilience, New York City[11]

The New York metropolitan area is home to almost 20 million people and a large number of small- and medium-sized businesses as well as multinational corporations. Sitting at the hub of the global finance and trading systems, New York's interconnectedness is deep and global, creating vulnerabilities worldwide to disaster in New York City. Superstorm Sandy caused an estimated $50 billion in damage in 2012. The frequency of such extreme climatic events – including flooding, heat waves and tornadoes – is expected to increase because of climate change. Flood hazards that have occurred once every hundred years are projected to occur at a frequency of once every fifteen, for example. The resilience of New York City is a concern for citizens and public agencies, but also for business, whether operating locally or globally.

11   The City of New York (2013)

> In the aftermath of Superstorm Sandy, New York City worked with federal and state agencies and consulted with community organisations and businesses to produce a resilience plan for the city. The plan prioritises actions needed to build resilience in vulnerable parts of the city, including coastal protection actions, amendments to zoning and building codes, retrofitting of buildings for wind and flood resilience, insurance initiatives and changes to infrastructure and organisation for healthcare, telecommunications, electrical utilities, water and wastewater and transportation. Assessments carried out by engineering companies have identified how to build the resilience of critical infrastructure such as the electrical grid. They identify options for making the grid more robust, using technologies for flood-proofing but also programmes for reducing energy demand by voluntary means and eventually advanced energy management systems. At the same time, New York City's plans call for a focus on strengthening individuals and groups able to organise and mobilise responses at local level, to help get people back to their homes quickly after disruptive events.

After the shock of Superstorm Sandy, New York City has begun making changes needed to strengthen resilience, by using a planning process to build a vision and engage communities and businesses. Citizen organisation is being combined with new government policies and regulations that create demand for services from companies that can help. New York City is contributing these lessons and others from their post-storm responses to the Rockefeller Foundation's 100 Resilient Cities initiative, which provides city authorities access to a wide network of cities with a similar framing of the issues, with a view to developing and sharing new solutions.

In Wallowa County, Oregon, local innovation for resilience emerged from collaboration. Here, civil society and local government collaborated not only to restore a badly degraded ecosystem, but also to rebuild the business climate and the community's social fabric, locally at least.

Case 3 – Timber Industry Reorganisation and Transformation, Wallowa County, Oregon, USA[12]

The listing of Chinook salmon under the Endangered Species Act in north-east Oregon led to near cessation of timber harvesting in the Wallowa-Whitman National Forest (WWNF) in 1992. Sawmills closed and WWNF revenue declined by 98%. In addition to jobs lost in the timber industry, staffing of the WWNF was

---

12   Jones and Christoffersen (2013)

cut by 50%, leading to removal of the forest management regime and a decline in forest health. Pest infestation and high-intensity fires caused extensive forest die-off.

To lead reorganisation and innovation for resilience, local government and local citizens formed Wallowa Resources, a non-profit organisation, in 1996. The organisation implements programmes in watershed restoration and research and education on community stewardship, while running a for-profit company to provide capital and business development services for local forest-based companies. Wallowa Resources restored the salmon and trout habitat and 80,000 ha of watershed. It installed micro-hydro and biomass power generators. It also succeeded in restarting commercial timber operations through collabora-tive agreements among the state, communities and local business.

Local governments, businesses and citizens have led an innovation process in Wallowa County and rescued a community. The scale of impact remains modest, however, relative to the potential of the forest resources available. Policy and law at higher levels, as well as environmental NGOs, are trapped in a use versus no-use debate that works against large-scale reorganisation and is a disincentive to corporate investment. Collaboration and empower-ing people to take action were key to unlocking the processes of change at local scale, but their absence at higher scales may be blocking the 'bounce forward' needed for the region's forest-based economy.

Applying collaboration to resilience

Working together, business, government and civil society can create changes in institutions, decision-making and investment that they cannot achieve alone, with results for conservation, community development and enter-prise profitability. They can create conditions in which businesses that avoid environmental impacts and create broader social value are favoured – in the market, through regulations and incentives and in terms of legitimacy with stakeholders. In systems terms, by working in collaboration they build feedbacks that guide each sector in shaping change and innovation.

Does multi-sector collaboration provide leverage on change in complex systems that will help companies as well as communities and countries build resilience? The test comes in understanding how collaboration contributes to building blocks needed for resilience – including diversity, infrastructure and technologies, distributed governance and learning.

Resilience benefits from diversity in, for example, value chains and markets, production methods and employees, as well as nature and infrastructure. With diversity, an enterprise can switch to an alternate supply chain in case of disruption, while diverse teams foster innovation and creativity. The same logic applies outside a business, as diversity in, for example, energy supply or transportation systems buffer populations and the broader economy against disruption. Diversity in nature helps to sustain services from ecosystems – including water cycling, soil conservation or coastal stability – needed in supply chains, for food security or for reducing disaster risk.

Collaboration enhances diversity. It brings a variety of players together to work on problem solving and change. Working collectively they bring variation in resources, including financial, social and natural capital. Business can provide managerial expertise and financing streams, while civil society can mobilise communities quickly with grassroots knowledge. From collaboration, a wider range of options and ideas may emerge for responding to stresses and disruptions, including options that work at local level, closer to impacts, that may be alternatives to or coordinated with actions at higher scales.

Case 4 – Restoring Resilience in Shinyanga Region, Tanzania[13]

From the 1950s to the 1980s, woodlands were cleared in semi-arid Shinyanga Region, north-west Tanzania, to eradicate the tsetse fly and to open land for agricultural cash cropping. By 1985, the region was declared the 'desert of Tanzania' by President Nyere, with the agro-pastoralist Sukuma people in the region vulnerable to water and fuel wood shortages and suffering declining productivity because of soil erosion and scarcity of dry season forage for livestock.

Reversing its previous top-down policy, government introduced a landscape restoration programme that resurrected traditional local management institutions. Working with local people, district government and NGOs, these mobilised local knowledge on woodland management through participatory planning to restore ngitili, or enclosed woodland reserves. By 2004, approximately 300,000 ha of ngitili had been restored. The multiplicity of goods (fuel, building timber, fruits, fodder, medicines) from the ngitili spread the risk of cash crop failure, and better watershed condition improved water availability using natural infrastructure. Communities reorganised and rebuilt to become more food, energy and water secure.

13   Barrow (2013)

Infrastructure and technologies contribute to resilience where, for example, they are sustainable and robust, with wide tolerances and incorporating ecosystem functioning, and that continue to operate in spite of climatic extremes or service outages. Transportation systems protected from flooding, for example, electrical grids with extra capacity and redundancy, or water treatment facilities that can be restarted quickly after major storms. Infrastructure and technologies likewise need to be sustainable, not undercutting adaptive capacity by contributing to social disruption or loss of system diversity or biodiversity.

Working together, governments, civil society and business may have more success in ensuring that technology choices are robust because they can have a deeper understanding through collaboration of the breadth of stresses that need to be taken into account and their impacts at different scales. Jointly, they may identify packages of infrastructure and technologies, including their operations and use of ecosystems as natural infrastructure, that avoid social disruption or environmental impacts and contribute to adaptive capacity.

Case 5 – Urban Drought Resilience, Gold Coast, Australia[14]

Between the mid-1990s and 2010, Australia contended with the 'Millennium Drought', said to be the driest period since European settlement. Although Australia is a country used to living with periodic water scarcity, this led Australians and Australian governments to rethink the way water is used and managed. There is broad recognition that significant components of the Australian economy are vulnerable to drought, certainly agriculture, but also the main urban centres. With climate change in mind, major steps are underway – including many that are highly contested – to change how water allocations are prioritised, to introduce much greater flexibility in responding to drought, and to cut water demand. Cities are leading the way by applying 'water-sensitive urban design' to reducing vulnerabilities to drought.

The city of Gold Coast in south-east Queensland, has relied on the Hinze Dam for its primary source of drinking water, but with the population in the region projected to grow from 400,000 to 1.1 million by 2050, climate-resilient alternatives are needed. As part of its response, the city council called for a 'Water Futures Master Plan' for a new housing development at Coomera Waters in the mid-2000s. The challenge was to transform conventional urban water systems

14   Davis and Farrelly (2009)

in Coomera Waters. The council put together a project team comprising a mix
of council staff and seconded personnel from industry who worked together to
build participation by stakeholders in the process, including housing developers,
construction trades, resident associations, environmental groups and other parts
of government. The final plan integrated rainwater harvesting, dual water supply
to households (potable and recycled grey water), 'smart' storm water management and sewerage, natural infrastructure (restored and artificial wetlands),
demand management and community education. Serving 150,000 people over a
7,000 ha site, the plan is projected to reduce use of potable water by 84%.

Participants in the project identified collaboration among both professionals and stakeholders as key to overcoming regulatory and approval barriers
and to learning that led council staff to become catalysts for change in their
organisation. The project created the space needed for a cross-disciplinary and
inter-institutional collaborative team to innovate and experiment, not only with
engineering, but also social and regulatory change. Coomera Waters will as a
result be less vulnerable to drought than older suburbs reliant on the dam.

Distributed governance, with decentralised decision-making at different
levels connected through networks rather than a single, top-down centre
of authority, aids resilience. Provided that responsibilities and boundaries
of authority are clear and defined, responses to shocks and stresses can be
identified independently and implemented rapidly at the most effective
level, and coordinated and communicated through networks. Whether
in a company or, for example, in a river basin trying to cope with water
scarcity, decision-making is then agile and the governance system itself
can adapt to change. Decentralisation and participation in decision-making
generates the capacity to self-organise and dynamically reorganise, both
critical to resilience.

Where business and governments collaborate with civil society organisations that work with stakeholders, they can increase participation, including
participation in networks. Those closest to the impacts of stresses and
disruptions can then shape and define solutions to vulnerabilities. They can
also come to consensus on who is responsible for different types of decisions
and at which levels, while using networks to communicate and coordinate.

Finally, learning and access to information and knowledge are fundamental to resilience. Companies, communities or public agencies can adjust
their actions or redesign their operations more readily and in a more timely
way if people are consistently learning and have the capacities to locate
new data and information and then appropriately apply new knowledge.
By using scenario planning, for example, they gain foresight capacity and

an improved chance of detecting and reducing emerging vulnerabilities. Adaptiveness and innovation is strengthened further with scope to experiment, learn and adjust.

Working jointly, business, governments and civil society can develop new knowledge networks that provide more channels for learning and for acquiring and sharing data and information. They have more opportunities to experiment, learn collectively from success and failure and to then adjust or reorganise accordingly. Through collaboration and knowledge networks they can put in place feedback loops that enable faster responsiveness to new information that is then applied more effectively.

Conclusion: A collaborative agenda for resilience

This chapter is the result of a cross-sector reflection on the topic of collaboration. Under a grant from the Rockefeller Foundation, IUCN convened a group of individuals from business (the Resilience Action Initiative companies), NGOs and government to discuss how the resilience lens impacts the collaboration agenda.

Business, government and civil society are increasingly recognising that they must learn to operate in a more turbulent world. Each is contemplating a future where planetary boundaries, global interconnectedness and converging stresses will make disruptions and instabilities more common. Each faces the same fundamental challenge – that to be resilient they will need adaptive capacities to survive, reorganise, learn and improve within the complex social and ecological systems in which they are embedded. Each sector therefore has a stake in innovation for resilience.

Innovation for resilience needs to provoke and steer transformations beyond technological change to address social change that will reinforce adaptive capacities and safeguard benefits from natural systems. There are echoes from organisational change in this challenge, as success is more apparent where change incorporates social processes that reshape norms. Collaboration, empowerment to take action and learning are key in organisational change, but they are also critical to influencing and leveraging deeper change in social-ecological systems and to reinforcing building blocks for resilience.

There are contributions to be made by each of the private and public sectors and civil society to the building blocks of resilience. Knowledge of how to translate principles into either practical action or guiding strategies and policies is not well developed or widely shared. Lessons are, however, emerging from a variety of cases in which change is demonstrated in response to vulnerabilities or collapse that combines elements of, for example, community action, innovation in programmes of local or national governments, or new services and leadership from business. These contributions reflect the interests of each sector in resilience, but also the potential of using collaboration among sectors to more effectively achieve results.

Businesses, governments and civil society are just beginning to discover where there is mutual advantage in collaboration on resilience. A collaborative resilience agenda that focuses on well-defined, practical problems will help to activate change and accelerate progress. Institutions and individuals who can act as brokers and facilitators to bring the sectors together are needed, not least to help build a common understanding of resilience and a common language that is shared by all sectors. They should work with leaders from the sectors to champion change needed for resilience and to promote learning from practical experiments with resilience that show results. Better metrics for resilience and diagnostics that will enable comparisons and monitoring of changes will help further. Finally, a collaborative resilience agenda should put in place networks that will share and elevate successful resilience practice for the scaling up of change, supported by partnerships that are able to leverage the needed knowledge, resources and financing.

5   Building resilience through teamwork

Seven tips to make it work[1]

Marco Albani[2] and Kimberly Henderson[3]

Resilience often challenges cross-jurisdictional boundaries and require systemic changes beyond the capabilities of individual companies or even of an entire industry. In these cases, the best approach for business can be to partner up – with governments, investors, local communities, non-governmental organisations (NGOs), and other companies. Think of these partnerships as distinctive and complicated joint ventures, often with multiple parties.

Such collaborations often go through phases – good, bad, and sometimes ugly, particularly in the early days. In its first few years, the Marine Stewardship Council, a partnership that sets standards for the fishing industry, struggled with high staff turnover and unstable funding. In the past decade, however, it has become a force. Its certification standards cover 10 per cent of the global seafood harvest and almost a quarter of global shoppers recognise the MSC label. This covers more than 20,000 products, sold in over 100 countries.

To understand how to make these collaborations work, McKinsey & Co. has interviewed dozens of business, government, and NGO leaders. From this research, we have identified seven essential principles of success.

1.   Identify clear reasons to collaborate

> "The effort needs to help each partner organisation achieve something significant. Incentives such as, 'we'll do this for good publicity,' or 'we don't want to be left out', are not sufficient."
> *Nigel Twose, director of the Development Impact Department, International Finance Corporation, World Bank Group*

---

1   A version of this chapter appears in the summer 2014 issue of McKinsey on Sustainability and Resource Productivity.
2   Senior Expert in the Sustainability and Resource Productivity Practice of McKinsey & Company
3   Consultant in McKinsey & Company's London office.

When organisations sign up for a sustainability partnership simply because they don't want to say no or be left out, commitment can be weak. Founders of a nascent partnership must instead identify strong incentives, such as maintaining a licence to operate, or ensuring the long-term endurance of a profitable resource or input, such as fish stocks, clean water, or forests. If participants cannot pinpoint such motivations, that may be a sign that the mission is ill-defined.

Any collaboration must make sense for all parties, whether their primary interests are commercial, environmental, or social. Enlightened self-interest is the only genuinely sustainable motive. That was certainly true for the firms that set up COSIA, the Canada Oil Sands' Innovation Alliance. This is an alliance of companies that mine oil out of Canada's bituminous sands; their goal is to share R&D in order to improve the environmental performance of an industry that is the subject of significant public debate.

Sometimes external events can force different players to acknowledge that change is necessary. The collapse of the North Atlantic's Grand Banks cod fisheries in the early 1990s made commercial fisheries much more interested in sustainable harvesting practices, laying the ground for the birth of the Marine Stewardship Council.

A small problem can be more difficult to collaborate around than a big one, because the reward for solving it does not excite people or justify the effort involved. It also helps to stay in the limelight. Although no one should join a collaboration just for PR reasons, publicity and progress can go hand-in-hand. Attention can bring more support, add credibility, and generate momentum.

A partnership to improve agriculture practices in Africa seems to be off to a good start in this regard. In 2011, the World Economic Forum worked with the African Union to create Grow Africa, a public-private partnership platform focused on increasing private investment in African agriculture. And in 2012, US President Barack Obama threw the G8's weight behind this partnership approach for African agriculture by announcing the New Alliance for Food Security and Nutrition. By the end of 2012, the G8's New Alliance and Grow Africa worked closely to secure over 3 billion dollars in private-sector investment commitments from nearly 50 local and global companies.

2.   Identify a 'fairy godmother'

"It is important to have a core of totally committed, knowledgeable people who would die in a ditch for what the organisation is trying to achieve."

Environmental NGO campaign head

Behind most successful collaborations are one or more organisations that are willing to invest more than their share of financial, human, and political capital to make the effort a success. Coordinated action can be difficult because first-movers take the biggest risks, while later entrants can benefit without much investment at all. So the temptation is to come in late. But someone has to start, or nothing will happen. 'Fairy godmothers' stop that from happening. They take on much of the risk and provide the generosity and sheer force of will that helps to build trust.

Any high-performing, credible institution may be a fairy godmother, as long as it is passionate, credible, and courageous. GE's CEO, Jeff Immelt, took on this role for the US Climate Action Partnership in 2007, driving the start-up phase and recruiting other companies to join.

3.   Set simple, credible goals

> "They [the NGO and the private sector] had different motives, but the same objective: Ensure sustainable fish stocks."
> *Antony Burgmans, former chairman and CEO of Unilever; co-founder of the Marine Stewardship Council (MSC)*

One certain way for a collaboration to stall is when the partners have different agendas. To guard against this, set an aspirational goal that everyone agrees on—and, preferably, one that could fit neatly on a bumper sticker. The collaboration should be anchored on an exciting, big idea, and create a vision that others will mobilise behind. Don't be afraid that it could also mobilise opposition; if there is no pushback, that may be a sign that the goal is not ambitious enough.

The MSC shows how this can work. The MSC started as a collaboration between Unilever and the World Wildlife Fund (WWF) in 1997; at the time, Unilever was the world's largest fish retailer. Each organisation faced challenges in starting the partnership. Some non-profits criticised the WWF for, in their opinion, compromising itself by working with a multinational. Unilever's leadership was divided on whether this was a good idea. Many fishing companies, and some governments, opposed developing marine sustainability standards.

Still, with leaders from both the WWF and Unilever committed to a clear goal of encouraging sustainable fishing practices, the project went ahead. The partners, using the successful Forest Stewardship Council (FSC) as an example, started by consulting with stakeholders, such as commercial fishermen, governments, and environmental organisations. Only then did they design the standards for what constituted sustainable fishing practices and seafood traceability; these are reviewed on a regular basis. In 1999, the MSC began operating as an independent non-profit, free of Unilever's and WWF's control.

4.   Get professional help

> "It is very important to have an honest broker. The facilitator must be neutral and very structured and keep people moving along at a brutal pace. You need someone who can bring things to a close."
>
> *Darrel Webber, Secretary General, RSPO*

Most collaborations need a facilitator to get started. When organisations come together, they each have their own incentives, biases, and organisational cultures. These can clash. Odds of conflict are highest when the organisations are either competitors or when they are from completely different sectors and cultures. The first few months tend to be particularly rough. Members are often slow to commit staff, and the tendency is to wait for others to offer resources first. By pooling funds for a facilitator, the collaboration can progress, even when staffing is still under negotiation.

In establishing the certification standard for palm oil, for example, the Roundtable for Sustainable Palm Oil (RSPO) needed to create a consensus among seven distinct interest groups, ranging from environmental non-profits to palm growers. It took two years of negotiation to develop RSPO's first standard. In reflecting on the arduous process, RSPO 's chief executive credited the independent, third-party facilitator with keeping the discussions (even heated ones) going until the parties could find common ground.

Over time, as trust and confidence builds and as the group moves from design to institutionalisation, a successful collaboration can and should phase out the facilitator. Ideally, individuals who started out as representatives of companies with competing interests become a cohesive group working toward a common goal.

5.   Dedicate good people to the cause

> "If a company like ours believes something is strategic,
> then we resource it like it is strategic."
> *Neil Hawkins, corporate vice president of sustainability, Dow Chemical*

If member organisations decline to dedicate qualified staff, check those organizations against point 1, and ask why they are in the collaboration. If good people are not volunteering, then check against points 2 and 3. Point 2 gives people security: They have a fairy godmother. Point 3 gives people clarity: They know what they're meant to do, and that it's worth doing. Working on a major collaboration should be an exciting career-builder, not a dead end. The collaboration's vision is particularly important at the beginning, when the effort is like a start-up. Talented individuals will give their all when they believe in the goals. As one of the participants of the US Climate Action Partnership said, "If I were to put anything on my tombstone, it would be this effort."

Internally, it's important to dedicate senior leadership. Without leadership, middle management often lack the incentive to take action, as well as the necessary decision-making power. Instead, they tend to favour business as usual. Cross-sector collaborations are inherently 'business as unusual'. Successful collaborations, at least at the start, are led by senior leaders from the founding organisations. When Yara, a Norwegian fertilizer company, agreed to become co-chair of Grow Africa, it dedicated a senior vice president to the role, and supported it with the sustained public engagement of its CEO.

6.   Be flexible in defining success

> "Partners think that collaboration will change the world. Then it doesn't, and
> they think that it failed. But often the collaboration changed something – the
> way some part of the system works and delivers outcomes. It is a matter of under-
> standing the nature of change itself."
> *Simon Zadek, visiting fellow, Tsinghua School of Economics and Management,*
> *Beijing*

Success may come from unexpected directions. Be ready to embrace, and build on it.

The US Climate Action Partnership (CAP) set out to pass national cap-and-trade legislation. While that did not happen, 11 US states have instituted such systems, and many other countries are implementing or considering them. Is any of this directly attributable to US CAP? No. Did US CAP help to pave the way, through developing a business-friendly approach? Quite likely.

Similarly, the MSC is changing the fishing industry beyond the 10% of fisheries that have signed up. A multitude of NGOs and other actors are working with fisheries that may never achieve the gold standard of MSC certification, but are nonetheless improving their practices.

So remember, while your collaboration may not change the world in precisely the way you intend, it can still change the rules of the game in a positive way.

7.   Prepare to let go

> "I've been absent from the FSC since 1997. The organisation had been born and was a teenager and needed to go off and find a job and do its own work."
> *NGO campaign head during the formation of the Forest Stewardship Council*

At some point, the partnership will either wind down, or become an independent entity. That process should be planned for.

Some collaborations are designed to achieve a certain objective. Once that objective has been achieved, or once the window for achieving it has closed, it's time to shut the doors. No collaboration should be kept alive beyond its useful lifetime.

Others evolve into permanent, self-sustaining, and independent institutions, such as the Forest Stewardship Council. In these cases, founders typically move out of the picture once both a long-term funding model is in place and there is a capable leader on the job. Like good parenting, you know you've succeeded when you are a welcome visitor, but you are clearly no longer needed on a day-to-day basis.

Part III
Resilience in action

6   The case for green infrastructure

Neil C. Hawkins[1] and Glenn Prickett[2]

Green infrastructure (GI) was investigated as part of a joint-industry programme that aimed to find ways to increase business resilience to external economic and environmental stressors. For the purposes of this study, GI solutions are defined as planned and managed natural and semi-natural systems that can provide more categories of benefits, when compared to traditional *gray* infrastructure. Experts from the Dow Chemical Company, Shell, Swiss Re and Unilever, working with The Nature Conservancy and a resilience expert,[3] evaluated a number of business case studies, and developed recommendations that green and hybrid infrastructure solutions should become part of the standard toolkit for modern engineers.

Green infrastructure employs elements of natural systems, while traditional gray infrastructure is man-made. Examples of green infrastructure include creating oyster reefs for coastal protection, and reed beds that treat industrial waste water, and restoring natural riparian habitat to enhance water provision.

The research team evaluated the assumption that green infrastructure can provide more opportunities than gray infrastructure to increase the resilience of industrial business operations against disruptive events such as mechanical failure, power interruption, raw material price increases, and floods. The evaluation concluded that hybrid approaches, utilizing a combination of green and gray infrastructure, may provide an optimum solution to a variety of shocks and improve the overall business resilience.

The case studies gathered to support this research encompass a wide array of possible applications of green infrastructure. They range from planting trees that cost-effectively remediate contaminated soil (phytoremediation), to constructing wetlands that naturally treat industrial wastewater, to mitigating air pollution through innovative forest-management approaches. The hope is this work will influence fellow companies and organisations to pursue green and/or hybrid solutions when financially appropriate.

1   Corporate Vice President Sustainability, Dow Chemical Company
2   Chief External Affairs Officer, The Nature Conservancy
3   Roland Kupers was an advisor to the green infrastructure work.

Introduction and objective

The global economy is a tightly wound system, extremely interconnected and efficient, with increasing risks to organisations due to the rapid propagation of disruptive events. Ecosystem services, the goods and services humans receive from nature, underpin the global economy and provide tremendous value to people and organisations. Receiving services from nature is often more cost-effective and sustainable than generating them with man-made materials like steel and concrete. The assumption that the research team sought to test is that working together with natural systems, and hence green infrastructure, enables organisations to better manage disruptive events, such as power interruption, raw material price increases and mechanical failure which often impair traditional gray solutions.

The focus of this study was to evaluate the ability of GI solutions to increase the resilience of industrial business operations to external stressors, to enhance the economic protection of business assets and infrastructure and to reduce the resource intensity in the context of the globally applicable energy-water-food nexus.

The GI team evaluated a number of business case studies from their respective organisations and from literature where GI solutions have been or may be implemented. The team interviewed 14 project leaders to assess the level of resilience each project had to acute, chronic and social stressors as well as a comparison to the traditional gray alternative. Where data was not available for direct comparison, informed judgments from subject matter experts were used. The team published a joint-industry White Paper entitled *The Case for Green Infrastructure*, which includes distilled findings from the interviews and subsequent evaluation of the assumption as stated above.[4]

The key business case studies that the team evaluated were based on interviews with project leaders and are listed below. More detailed information can be found on each case study in the appendix.

1. Dow: Phytoremediation for Groundwater Decontamination, Ontario, Canada
2. Dow: Constructed Wetlands for Waste Water Treatment, Texas, USA
3. Dow & TNC: Air Pollution Mitigation via Reforestation, Texas, USA
4. Shell: Produced Water Treatment Using Reed Beds, Nimr, Oman
5. Shell: Natural Reclamation and Erosion Control for Onshore Pipelines, NE British Columbia, Canada

---

4   http://www.nature.org/about-us/working-with-companies/companies-we-work-with/
building-a-case-for-green-infrastructure.xml

6. Shell & TNC: Coastal Pipeline Erosion Control Using Oyster Reefs, Louisiana, USA
7. TNC: Cauca Valley Water Fund, Cali, Colombia
8. TNC: Integrated Reservoir Floodplain Management, Georgia and South Carolina, USA
9. TNC: Managing Storm Water Runoff with Wetlands, Philadelphia, PA, USA
10. TNC: Oyster Reef Building & Restoration for Coastal Protection, Louisiana, Mississippi and Alabama, USA

The remainder of the chapter highlights the pros and cons of green (natural) and gray (man-made) solutions and proposes innovative approaches to balance the different trade-offs involved when designing resilient infrastructure.

Green infrastructure: Concept and definition

GI solutions are defined, for the purpose of this study, as planned and managed natural and semi-natural systems which can provide more categories of benefits, when compared to traditional gray infrastructure. GI solutions can enhance or even replace a functionality that is traditionally provided by man-made structures.

GI solutions aim to build upon the success that nature has had in evolving systems that are inherently sustainable and resilient. GI solutions employ ecosystem services to create more resource-efficient systems involving water, air and land use. GI solutions are designed to fulfil a specific need, such as water purification or carbon sequestration, while often offering location-specific and valuable co-benefits, such as enhanced habitat for wildlife.

Green infrastructure: Solution examples

The business case studies varied from a private entity solving a water treatment challenge within its fence line to a multi-stakeholder organisation working together with a city to create a storm water management programme, to a conservation organisation working with governments and communities on coastal erosion control. Four GI solutions, describing the recurring benefits and challenges inherent to GI solutions are described below. They set the stage for subsequent discussions on the trade-offs involved when designing green or hybrid infrastructure solutions.

Union Carbide Corporation, subsidiary of the Dow Chemical Company
Seadrift, TX, Wetlands for Wastewater Treatment
Project description: 110-acre engineered wetlands in lieu of an industrial wastewater treatment plant
In 1995, the Seadrift water treatment facility was seeking a solution to consistently meet regulatory requirements for water discharge. An innovative GI solution consisting of a constructed wetlands was installed and has been successfully operating upon startup and for the last 15 years. The constructed wetlands design offered the following advantages and disadvantages:

Advantages:
– **Capital expense savings**: $1.2-1.4 million versus $40 million for the gray infrastructure alternative proposed
– **Operating expense savings**: No energy, additives, or oxygen; no biosolids disposal; minimal maintenance
– **Lower environmental footprint**: Eliminated the need for the construction and operation of an energy-intensive wastewater treatment facility
– **Labour reduction**: Operational support drastically different; a wetland requires minimal support from operations and maintenance as opposed to the gray alternative requiring 24/7 support
– **Operational performance**: 100% compliant upon startup and for over 15 years
– **Construction benefits**: Project implementation time reduced by half (fully operational in 18 months)
– **Other benefits**: Provides habitat for deer, bobcats, and birds; educational opportunities for local schools

Disadvantages:
– **On-site large project land footprint**: 110 acres as opposed to 4-5 acres for a *gray* infrastructure alternative
– **1-2 year pilot period**: Required to de-risk the GI technology and find the optimum design
– **Criteria for application of this solution**: Compliance with applicable regulations related to water quality
– **Biotic stresses**: Relatively minor disturbances that the system had to overcome (nutria invasion, alligators, etc.)

Petroleum Development Oman LLC (PDO): Constructed Wetlands for
Produced Water Treatment, Oman
Project description: More than 360 ha engineered wetland in lieu of disposing
water in deep aquifers
The need to manage large amounts of produced water created a major
limiting factor for the oil production from the Nimr fields, in which the
Shell Petroleum Company Ltd is a joint venture partner. These large volumes
would normally require an extensive water processing infrastructure to
treat and inject the water into a deep disposal well. Man-made infrastructure would thus result in a high cost facility requiring large amounts of
electric power and producing greenhouse gas emissions.

The PDO team investigated alternative, low-cost solutions to treat and
dispose of the water. The world's largest commercial wetlands treats more
than 30 vol% (95,000 m³ per day) of the total produced water from the Nimr
oilfields in Oman. The four-tier gravity-based wetlands design offered the
following advantages and disadvantages:

Advantages:
- **Capital expense savings**: Significant capital cost savings compared to
  the man-made water treatment and injection facility
- **Operating expense savings**: Power consumption reduced by approximately 98% due to the elimination of electric-powered water treatment
  and injection equipment
- **Operational performance**: Satisfactory water treatment performance
  ever since the start of the wetlands operation (December 2010). The oil
  content in the produced water is consistently reduced from 400 mg/l to
  less than 0.5 mg/l when leaving the wetlands system
- **Significantly reduced carbon footprint**: CO_2 emissions reduced by
  approximately 98% due to the elimination of electric-powered water
  treatment and injection equipment
- **Other benefits**: The wetlands provide habitat for fish and hundreds
  of species of migratory birds. Also, the wetlands offer potential for innovative customer value propositions that could provide a variety of
  socio-political benefits, e.g. through byproduct optimisation (fresh water,
  biomass, etc.)

Disadvantages:
- **Large required land footprint**: More than 360 ha to treat 95,000 m³ per
  day of produced water

- **Long pilot period (>2 years):** Required to de-risk the constructed wetlands technology and find the optimum wetlands design
- **Operational risk of the wetlands:** Potential risk of not meeting the performance requirements due to external factors (e.g. seasonal temperature swings, biotic stresses)

The Dow Chemical Company: Phytoremediation for Groundwater Decontamination, Sarnia, Ontario, Canada
Project description: Trees mitigating groundwater contamination
Phytoremediation is the engineered use of green plants to remove, contain, stabilise or destroy contaminants in the soil and groundwater. The uptake of groundwater by the plants can achieve containment of the groundwater and contamination (trees are basically acting as a solar pumps). Engineered planted systems can degrade, extract and control the groundwater contamination.

One specific installation was completed at the Dow Sarnia facility. This large industrial complex contained several manufacturing units that operated for more than 60 years. The effort in ceasing operations included transitioning the existing traditional pump and treat groundwater treatment system. The traditional system consisted of pumping groundwater via carbon beds prior to transferring the recovered groundwater to an external water treatment facility.

While still operating the pump and treat facility, the site was prepared by minimising external infiltration and planting 1,300 trees (poplar and willows) on an area of roughly two acres to handle the uptake of the groundwater. As the trees grow along with site hydrology adaptation, some of the water still needs to be pumped and treated during this transition period. This technology does require ongoing site maintenance such as sampling and analysis of ground water, hydrology testing to ensure ground water is contained, and tree management over the life of the project.

Advantages:
- No wastewater needing to be transported off site in trucks
- No electricity required
- Elimination of the carbon filtration system and expense related to its operation and disposal of spent carbon
- No need for 24/7 hour operation (from an operation to a management activity)
- Significant reduction in maintenance costs compared to pump and treat

Disadvantages:
- Higher level of uncertainty at the onset of the project since dealing with a biological system, local geology, contaminants, site hydrology
- Larger physical footprint than the gray alternative
- Requires a period of growth to come to full operation
- Try to limit interaction with biota since concerns with creating a wildlife habitat within a remediation site
- Different set of challenges to deal with requiring different set of skills such as dealing with main disturbance (e.g. rabbits eating tree bark)
- Ensure that tight feedback and monitoring systems are in place to alleviate any environmental concern (e.g. leaves/pollen off the trees)

Shell Canada Limited: Natural Reclamation and Erosion Control for Onshore Pipelines
Project description: Reclamation along pipelines in British Columbia
Shell's projects often involve the construction of pipeline corridors in ecologically diverse areas on previously undeveloped lands called 'greenfield' development. The pipeline is routed along what is known as a 'right of way'. When building a pipeline, the construction activities not only cover the civil works to lay the pipeline and build the pump/compressor stations, but also the reclamation work to return disturbed land to an equivalent land capability with minimal impact on the environment. There is heightened recognition and popularity of natural reclamation and soil erosion abatement techniques as these ancient techniques address the shortfalls related to man-made pipeline-protection techniques, particularly in terms of reduced installation and maintenance costs.

The technique of using living plant materials to create structures that perform some soil-related engineering function is referred to as soil 'bioengineering'. Often, soil bioengineering is used to treat sites where surface stability and erosion problems exist. Bioengineering solutions can be applied to a wide variety of sites disturbed by construction activities. These solutions use natural components of pioneering plant communities and thus align well with ecological restoration strategies.

It is preferred to use local plant species to construct soil bioengineering solutions for naturally disturbed sites. Some recent innovations in reclamation approaches include the use of willows and other tree/shrub/plant species to control soil erosion and establish a re-naturalisation path. In the past 15 years, Shell has proven success in willow staking in several upstream projects. Poplars and willows are highly valued for erosion control and efficient control of groundwater due to their rapid growth, high rooting capacity, extensive root systems and high water use.

Pipeline projects involve many stakeholders with specific interests and concerns. The pipeline right of way often traverses lands with rights of use belonging to multiple indigenous communities. The indigenous communities are often concerned with the fragmentation of the land and its impacts on the local ecosystem. Therefore, all solutions are strictly reviewed with these local concerns in mind.

Advantages:
- Lower overall environmental impact, potentially including CO_2 offsets
- Solutions are known to be superior over time compared to the more traditional stabilisation methods
- Hands-on work can be structured as a team-building/educational activity for Shell employees
- Job creation for local labour
- The solution can be designed to be sensitive to the local environment (e.g. allow access to local wildlife)
- These green solutions do not require regular maintenance as compared to gray solutions that often require mechanical intervention (e.g. for the excavation of existing banks or transport of materials)
- Low operating and maintenance cost

Disadvantages:
- Not a one-stop solution, but very much site specific (dependent on soil types, moisture level, light, etc.)
- Requires a different skill set for the design and implementation phase
- Time constraints: any project would need to be started as early in the winter as possible
- Survivability of the planting sites is an important requirement to establish long-term success

Identifying areas of opportunity

The key differences between green and gray infrastructure are summarised in Table 1 and illustrate the trade-offs involved when evaluating green versus gray solutions. These trade-offs help identify the specific areas of opportunity for optimum resilient infrastructure which are often combinations of new GI solutions integrated into existing facilities, creating so-called *hybrid solutions*. This evaluation and opportunity assessment was conducted during a meeting of the participating organisations.[5]

Evaluation criteria	Green infrastructure	Gray infrastructure
Stakeholder involvement	Extended stakeholders are often required to support the project and may have an active and ongoing role in the project design and operation	Stakeholders are often engaged with the aim to create local support for the project, but without active involvement in the project design and operation
Engineering approach	GI solutions require a custom-made, location-specific design and do not lend themselves to standardisation and replication	Traditional engineering solutions enable standardization and replication which can significantly reduce project costs and delivery times
Physical footprint	A large physical footprint is often required due to low energy density	Usually, only a small physical footprint is required due to high energy density
Environmental footprint	Often reduced environmental footprint due to GI solutions being nature-based and self-regenerating	Often increased environmental footprint due to material and energy intensive processes (manufacturing, distribution, operation)
Speed of delivering the functionality	GI solutions may take time (years) to grow to provide a certain service and capacity	Traditional engineering solutions provide a certain service and capacity from day 1 of operation
Susceptibility to external factors	GI solutions are susceptible to extreme weather conditions, seasonal changes in temperature or rainfall and disease	Gray infrastructure is susceptible to power loss, mechanical failure of industrial equipment and price volatility
Operational and maintenance costs	Operating and maintenance costs are often significantly lower (only monitoring and feedback is required)	Operating costs are often significantly higher due to power consumption, operational and maintenance requirements
Risk of price volatility	GI solutions are relatively insensitive to fluctuations in the cost of raw materials, oil, gas and power	Traditional engineering solutions are sensitive to fluctuations in the cost of raw materials, oil, gas and power
Approach to system monitoring and control	GI solutions are living and complex systems that can be monitored and effectively managed by a deep understanding of the key control variables	Traditional engineering solutions are man-made systems that are typically designed with established monitoring techniques to effectively manage and control system performance

5   Hawthorne, New York, October 2012

Evaluation criteria	Green infrastructure	Gray infrastructure
Required operating personnel	No need for 24/7 operational supervision	Complex control and safeguarding systems typically require 24/7 operational supervision
Expenses for increasing capacity of system	Relatively inexpensive to extend the capacity of the GI solution, provided there is physical footprint available	Extension of capacity could be relatively inexpensive as long as significant modification or redesign is not required
Need for recapitalisation	Recapitalisation during the life of the GI solution is usually not significant. The end-of-life replacement/decommissioning will vary greatly depending on the GI technology selected but is usually not necessary as GI solutions are self-sustaining and do not depreciate	Gray solutions are depreciating assets with a finite performance capacity and usually require significant replacement/decommissioning at end of life

Key conclusions

Assessments of a range of examples, some operating over more than a decade, have clearly demonstrated the role that green infrastructure can play within a portfolio of technology options. GI solutions form an essential element in a portfolio of solutions to increase the resilience of industrial business operations, but do not provide resilience against every potential stressor and therefore benefit from thorough site investigation and management of location specific risks. This is an important caveat when assessing the preferred option or combination of options for a specific situation.

The research team found that GI solutions often demonstrate financial advantages compared to gray infrastructure due to a reduction of both initial capital expenses and ongoing operational and maintenance expenses. GI solutions can also be used to strategically recapitalise aging assets.

While one might expect that these financial advantages would drive and reinforce use of GI technologies, our research indicates that this is often not the case. The lack of integration into technology capabilities, capital reviews or assessments, champions are required in today's organisations to investigate and drive these non-traditional, cost-advantaged solutions. Engineers build what they know. "It's hard to sell a swamp to an engineer", was a key message from one of the project team. GI solutions offer opportunities, often overlooked in current project assessments, to effectively manage socio-political risks through innovative collaboration with key stakeholders. Yet evaluation of the business case studies showed that a lack of expertise, lack of practical experience and other cultural barriers have hindered the full adoption of GI options with a variety of organisations. This is a critical dimension to address when integrating GI into evaluations of options and technologies. Failure to address this will result in missed opportunities and sub-optimal designs.

GI solutions often leverage existing natural resources. For example, as part of Shell's Natural Reclamation and Erosion Control for Onshore Pipelines project, local plant species are used to construct soil bioengineering solutions. Further, the regenerative processes of GI solutions consume less energy and are thus less sensitive to power loss and fluctuations in the cost of energy, as compared to gray infrastructure. This inherently adaptive capability of GI solutions can be very attractive to reduce ongoing operations and maintenance costs. While this might seem to confer an inherent resilience to GI options, it is not necessarily the case since both green and gray infrastructure resist shocks, but in different ways. *Hybrid* approaches, utilising a combination of green and gray infrastructure, may provide an optimum solution to improve the overall business resilience. Expertise and experience with both green and gray infrastructure options should be most likely to lead to the more resilient approach for any given project.

Organisations which hope to make the most of green infrastructure would be well served by the following considerations. They should employ a more comprehensive economic and environmental footprint analysis relative to traditional models and techniques to more accurately compare green versus gray infrastructure and to investigate, and when relevant, appropriately assess the co-benefits of GI solutions. GI solutions benefit from pilot projects and engagement of external partners to glean expertise, experiences and innovative approaches that can de-risk the GI solution and accelerate implementation. GI solutions invariably require organisations to engage in multi-stakeholder discussions. This is particularly true when building acceptance and consensus with regulators and local stakeholders who may benefit, or be impacted by, a GI project. Since organisations are currently not staffed with the requisite skills nor supported by the culture necessary to bring GI solutions to scale, this needs to be accounted for by either building capability in-house or leveraging others, including NGOs, who have the requisite expertise and experience. Leadership emphasis and change management is required for successful implementation. Through whatever combination of resources and expertise, organisations are advised to build a fit-for-purpose set of capabilities integrating the areas of strategy, innovation, new business development, project economics, engineering and environmental sustainability. Green infrastructure, as an underutilised capability, stands to enhance an organisation's resilience and provide financial benefits as well.

Moving forward

Dow has undertaken significant efforts to further the use of GI solutions within their operations. A concrete example is Dow's effort, as a first step in realising the business potential for green infrastructure, in ensuring that the proper tools are available to assess projects. A full retrospective analysis of the Seadrift constructed wetlands (CW) discussed above was performed using two conventional Dow tools, a replacement cost methodology for financial assessment and a life cycle assessment (LCA) for environmental impacts was completed and published in April 2014 in the *Journal of Industrial Ecology.* The Seadrift cost-benefit analysis yielded a net present value on the order of $200 million. The LCA showed clear advantages for the CW, based on its much lower use of electricity, chemicals, and capital.[6] Based on the success of this project, Dow has dedicated staff resources to evaluate opportunities to deploy green infrastructure solutions at sites around the globe, integrate GI solutions as part of its global project management process and create both an internal and external network of GI practitioners building knowledge and experience in this emerging field.

Additionally, Dow is working with The Nature Conservancy to continue to explore specific green infrastructure opportunities along with developing and testing methods for businesses to evaluate green infrastructure solutions alongside gray infrastructure solutions. The most promising result to date involves the progress made on the case study mentioned previously dealing with air pollution mitigation via reforestation in Texas, USA. The collaboration team is working with key stakeholders to seek approval of reforestation as a compliance measure for inclusion in the Texas State Implementation Plan (SIP) for ground-level ozone. Letters requesting consideration of the inclusion of reforestation in the Texas SIP have been submitted to the US EPA and the Texas Commission on Environmental Quality. If approval is granted, this could provide Dow and other companies based in Texas with the ability to consider large-scale reforestation as a method to help reduce components that form ozone. The evaluation tools

6   DiMuro et al. (2014)

developed to accomplish this pilot study should also be useful to other businesses.[7]

TNC is working to advance the current science and tools for incorporating GI into coastal hazard mitigation, inland flood risk reduction, urban water supply, as well as for improving water and air quality. TNC scientists, corporate practices and external affairs staff are working with engineering firms, reinsurers and other corporate partners to understand the opportunities as well as barriers to incorporating GI into corporations' plans for coastal and riverine natural hazard mitigation. As TNC and partners advance the science, tools, processes, policies, and market conditions needed to realise these opportunities, the results from such collaborations will enable corporations to enhance the resilience of their facilities by incorporating GI.

As a result of this study, RAI organisations have recognised the strategic importance of green infrastructure solutions and the need to include them among the suite of most effective technology options available to engineers.

7   Further details on this specific effort along with a complete summary of other efforts initiated by the collaboration between Dow and the Nature Conservancy can be found in The Nature Conservancy and Dow (2013).

7   Nexus! Resilience in a pressure cooker

Herman van der Meyden[1]

Nexus! is a board game simulation of an economy that faces energy, water and food stresses. The Resilience Action Initiative developed Nexus! to create an environment for experiential learning. The game energises participants ahead of discussions and allows an easy on-ramp to the somewhat abstract concept of resilience. It is a fun and interactive way to start engagements on the energy, water and food challenge for groups that are new to the topic. For experienced decision-makers, it provides good anchor points for reflection on cooperative behaviours. In a two-hour workshop, participants get to experience tough choices from the interconnections between resources, the resilience of growth strategies, as well as the challenges and opportunities of collaboration.

Nexus! has been designed to confront its players with a number of dilemmas that are at the heart of resilience, and give them a direct experience of dealing with the associated ambiguities:

– Resilience versus efficiency – Do I buy new assets as fast as I can or do I first build some buffers to guard against unforeseen events?
– Local sufficiency versus global trading – Do I try to produce all the resources I need within the boundaries of my own country or do I rely on the global market?
– Cooperation – Do I monopolise the available water to maximise my own use in the short term or do I cooperate to ensure a sustainable division of the available resource between all players?
– What is success? Players are told the winner will be the one with the most money at the end of the game, which players are free to interpret as maximising their personal wealth, or that of their game table.

The game development process

The developers of Nexus! have used a rapid-prototyping approach. The idea for the game was first conceived in January 2013. The final product was available in May of that year. In only four months, five different prototypes were built, tested and adjusted. Weekly tests were followed

1   Commercial advisor for Royal Dutch Shell in the Netherlands, and designer of Nexus!

by a fast evaluation of lessons learned and redesign. This approach combined rapid progress with the incorporation of views from many different stakeholders within the Resilience Action Initiative, who acted as test players.

Nexus! has drawn upon experience with the design of the Perspectivity Game,[2] a simulation of climate change dynamics. The team further took inspiration from games like Carcassonne, Settlers of Catan and Risk to design the fun factor into the game. In addition, it applied key concepts from the valuable game development guidebook "A Theory of Fun".[3] The element of simultaneous player decision-making, different from most turn-based games, was taken from Diplomacy. Lessons on social gaming were learned from the games Ökolopoly[4] and the Horn of Africa Risk Transfer for Adaptation (HARITA) project.[5] None of these existing games, however, combined the theme of energy, water and food resources with a design focused on resilience strategies and collaboration.

The game mechanics

In order to explain how resource interlinkages, resilience strategies and collaboration feature in Nexus!, let's start with the basic rule set. The game objective is simple: to make your economy grow. The participants play on a board with six teams, which ideally consist of two people each. An independent game leader acts as banker and runs the administration of the game economy.

The rules of Nexus! are quite simple and can be explained in less than ten minutes. Three of the teams play the governments of the imaginary countries Twengea, Miristan and Praland. The other three teams direct the games' companies. The countries are responsible for building and maintaining cities. The companies build farms, power plants and other infrastructure. The economic activities are interconnected through units of energy, water and food.

2   Perspectivity Game (www.perspectivity.org/game)
3   Koster (2005)
4   On Ökolopoly (Ecopoly – A Cybernetic Environment Game) and its author, Frederic Vester, a German biochemist and an expert in the field of ecology, see http://de.wikipedia.org/wiki/%C3%96kolopoly (in German).
5   IRI (2010)

While the rules are not very complicated, the game leader purposefully presents them at brisk pace during the 10-minute introduction. Most players really struggle to grasp them and are forced to start playing with a very limited understanding. In addition, the rules are not fixed and evolve during the game. These design elements put the players in a position where they need to deal with uncertainty. It makes applying simple tactics based on forecasting future developments next to impossible. This simulates the turbulent behaviour of systems at the energy-water-food nexus, and the often ambiguous 'rules of the game' in the real world.

A typical Nexus! player experience

Introduction: the game leader presents the set of rules at a rapid pace. All players struggle to keep up.

Round 1: Most players are frantically reading the rule card to find out what should be done. The first resources get traded. The players don't understand relative importance of resources. They just discover how the basic rules work.

Round 2: The plant virus disaster gets introduced to the game. The amount of rainwater that falls in the lake every round is announced. The quickest players already start formulating a deliberate strategy.

Round 3: Most players now grasp how trading works and what assets are available at the bank. The first resource scarcity appears. One country has now got full control over the lake water through pumps.

Round 4: Most players understand what's happening and have made a strategy. A water conference is organised, yet few players feel an urgency to negotiate about water.

Round 5: The first countries are falling behind on income. The game leader removes the first undersupplied city from the game board. Negotiations get more emotional.

Round 6: Most players now have fixed trading partners. There is very little of either energy or food in the entire game board. Players are bidding up the prices multiple times. There is short-term focus; strategising is very hard.

Round 7: The players hold a trade conference. Many proposals for multilateral collaboration are launched, but they cannot come to agreement.

Round 8: One country and one company are sensing that they are losing the game and start to get disillusioned. The leading players need the land and economies of the losers to grow further. The round information card announces the end of the game.

Round-up: While counting the scores: players start to reflect on the decisions made and start to grasp how their actions have shaped the outcome of the game. Some players start to justify their behaviour.

Debrief: The game leader links the game experience to resilience theory. Players reflect on alternative game results scenarios and what they could or perhaps should have done to achieve those.

Simulating aspects of resilience

The game concept and rules are further illustrated below in the context of the resilience frames introduced in Chapters 2 and 3. Additionally, the game highlights the essential value and importance of cross-sector collaboration. Nexus! incorporates aspects of five out of the nine lenses that were introduced in those chapters:
1. Innovation and experimentation
2. Redundancy
3. Requisite diversity
4. Social capital
5. Thresholds

1.   Innovation through research cards

Innovation is represented in Nexus! through research cards. The game leader explains during the introduction of the rules that research cards "may lead to asset improvements". As in the real world, the outcome of research is uncertain. When a player invests in research, she obtains a card with the research outcome, consisting of three variants: (1) dead-end, (2) biodiversity research success and (3) water efficiency research success.

 If the player gets the 'dead-end' card, then the money spent on research has not been productive. With the biodiversity card type, players can protect farms from a plant virus outbreak. The third card type allows participants to increase water-efficiency in farms, energy plants or cities. Because of the constrained amount of rainwater in the game, this obviously boosts the overall growth prospects.

2-3.   Resilience through redundancy and diversity

The game features a disastrous event in the form of the plant virus plague that causes harvests to fail. The occurrence of the plant virus represents a 'fat-tail event', rare but calamitous. Every round the participants need to spin the 'plant disease wheel' in the middle of the game board. This wheel hits one of the countries with a virus outbreak, which means that its farms will not produce anything in that round.

Companies can apply two measures to become resilient to the plant virus. The first measure involves 'innovation and experimentation' described above. The other option is to diversify their assets, by placing farms in different countries so that in any single round the impact of the plant virus is limited. The ability to realise this strategy depends on the willingness of the country players to allow investment in their territory.

The countries do not own farms themselves, since farming is solely the domain of the companies. The countries therefore have two different strategic options to improve the resilience against the plant virus. The first option is to create a small buffer of food, which is equivalent to redundancy in resilience terms. This buffer allows the country to always provide its cities with the food they need to survive, even when the virus strikes. Maintaining these buffers is clearly not the most efficient strategy, since the buffer can also be used to feed another city and generate higher returns. This introduces a trade-off in the game between efficiency and resilience. Countries can also become more resilient by striving for diversity in their supply chain by buying food from all three companies, instead of just their national supplier.

4.   Resilience through building social capital

One of the asset types that countries can build is a water pump. The function of the water pump is that it gives the country preferential control over the 'lake', the shared water resource in the middle of the game board. A pump needs energy in every round of the game in order to be active, just like a real pump requires electricity. The country that has the largest number of running water pumps has priority in extracting water from the lake. This country now has the power to extract all available water. It can then use its own share and sell back the remainder to other players. In other words, the country has the power to monopolise the water. Merely exercising this power once, normally triggers a race for other countries to also invest in water pumps and take over this monopoly.

After a number of game rounds, a new type of asset is introduced to the game: the desalination plant. When reasoned from an individual player's perspective, the water *pump* is a cheaper way to get access to water than this desalination plant. Collectively, however, the construction of water pumps follows the model of a classic arms race: The collective investment in water pump assets can easily go beyond the value of the water that is disputed; it becomes a zero-sum game.

The water in the lake is visually drawn in the centre of the game board and is naturally perceived as a public good. Its monopolisation invariably creates a hostile climate in the 'international relations' of the game. A country that monopolises the water and gets into trouble later, has seriously damaged goodwill from its fellow players. This brings in another aspect of resilience: transformative resilience through social capital. In the face of uncertainty about the game future, it is inherently valuable to maintain good relations with one's neighbours, which means sharing the lake water even when one has the power to monopolise it. This behaviour of being a responsible citizen fosters a cooperative climate where a country is much more likely to receive help when it is hit by unexpected negative events.

5.   Thresholds: Losing the last city

The cities in the game need to receive in every round at least a minimum amount of food and water to survive. When a country loses its second, third or fourth city, then it faces a 'linear' setback in the growth profile of its game economy. The player may afterwards save some resources or seek help from a company and invest in a new city. It is a loss, but the economic system boundaries within which the country operates do not really change.

On the contrary, when the country fails to provide minimum supply to its last city, an irreversible threshold is crossed. The country has now lost its value-creation potential. If left to its own devices, the country is doomed to end the game as a marginal player. The only way to get back into the game is foreign altruism, which is rare.

Awareness of systemic thresholds is an important step towards resilience. Country players in Nexus! generally identify the tipping point of losing the last city. When they get close, they try to influence corporate players to support them, to avoid passing the threshold. It is certainly in the rational interest of the company to support its home country, since also the company ultimately needs the money produced by cities. In the messy trading process, however, countries can really struggle to get this message of interdependence across.

Collaboration

Early in the game, time-outs are called for a water conference and then a trade conference. These conferences are designed into the game to provide players with an opportunity for collaboration. Experience shows that in most cases these opportunities are not utilised. It turns out to be difficult to centralise the attention of all 12 people around the game board. Mostly some players are distracted from the group discussion because they are working on their individual strategies.

On the other hand, player groups that do achieve a collective high-growth scenario typically lay a solid foundation during the conferences. Sometimes there is one participant with natural leadership who launches a proposal that immediately gets adopted by all parties. Other times, a coalition of three or four teams start with an agreement on water use, for example, and then coerce the remaining teams into compliance by threatening to stop trading with them.

Insights from a year of Nexus! sessions

The previous paragraphs describe five concepts of resilience that have been embedded in Nexus!. All of these concepts have been translated in very simple systems and logic, in order to make the game playable in an hour. Obviously, resilience strategies in real life are a lot more complex, with many more stakeholders involved, far larger asymmetries between them, as well as multi-scalar complexities. But modelling the real world is not the point of the game. The point is to provide an easy on-ramp to the concept of resilience, which for many is somewhat abstract and difficult to connect with. The debrief is therefore an integral part of the game. It is the moment where players see the relevance of their game experience for real life. The game leader's role is to help the players reach a higher level of understanding of what the resilience lens implies.

By early 2014, Nexus! had been played with a wide range of players, close to 2,000 participants in total, from students to executives, from public authorities to NGO representatives and academics.

Although the way the game is played varies a lot, some qualitative observations can be made from the behaviour of players across these sessions: The pressure from the speed of the game and the volatile business environment causes players to focus in a small circle. Most struggled to develop partnerships beyond their own local government or company. Often short-term considerations trumped the strategic view, with players ignoring innovation, not managing diversity and forgetting to keep buffers. Organisational culture matters: One group of NGO staff collectively opted for a maximum collaboration strategy; a group of young consultants on the other hand did the opposite by picking a take-no-prisoners strategy for maximum competition. Women were generally more inclined to spend time on a fair distribution of the common water resource. The tragedy of the commons, in this case the hoarding of the central water supply, typically needs only a single short-term focused player to materialise. Such action had a strong knock-on effect as collaboration on other issues also deteriorated rapidly thereafter. Finally it appears that success in the game is not much correlated to the level of education or professional development of the participants.

More important than the game outcomes, most participants have left the Nexus! sessions with a better appreciation of resource linkages, a deeper insight into resilience dynamics and richer reflections on how their individual behaviour can help shape systemic cooperation. It proves to do an excellent job in providing the intended fun on-ramp into the world of resilience theory.

8   Getting to resilience from the bottom-up

Thekla Teunis[1]

> Some people see the world as it is and ask: What can I do?
> Young people see the world as it could be and say: Together we can.
> – *Paul Polman, CEO of Unilever, paraphrasing George Bernard Shaw*[2]

Corporations as centrally governed structures themselves, have a tendency to view the world as being composed of large chunks. These chunks are in turn governed by authorities who establish policies and fund projects. When reflecting on resilience, the natural tendency is to focus on large projects that would enable a particular city or region to cope better with the stresses it may be exposed to. To complement this reflex towards top-down change, a project was initiated to explore how bottom-up projects might contribute as well. Young professionals from the Resilience Action Initiative (RAI) companies were invited to design and implement solutions to increase the resilience of the areas they are living and working in.

The project worked. As we have seen in several large cities in 2013, bottom-up initiatives can help corporates to find new business models for collaboration. The Resilience Action Initiative has sparked a movement of young professionals who act as local changemakers all over the world across company fence lines. Connecting people from different backgrounds and jointly generating action can help to build trust-based relationships locally. The skills, passion and expertise of young professionals can be leveraged to start and scale new collaborative business models addressing the energy-water-food challenges.

In Rotterdam young professionals finalised business cases and presented and launched three pilot projects, on the subjects of 'edible walls', a 'floating greenhouse' and 'clean driving'. The edible wall pilot has led to a spin-off company that will scale the concept, starting in Rotterdam. This success led to initiatives from young professionals elsewhere to set up similar projects.

---

1   Business developer at the Ecosystem Return Foundation in South Africa and Director Africa for the Land Life Company. Previously Thekla Teunis worked for Shell in Group Strategy, where she co-developed the RAI bottom-up programme.
2   Polman (2013)

Initiatives are underway in South Africa, the Philippines, and other cities in the Netherlands.

Next to selecting and identifying projects to increase resilience from the top, corporates can invite individuals from within companies to incubate a solution when there is a need and enthusiasm. This can become a bridge to move from global issues to real action on the ground, provided there is sufficient training and support. The focus should be on leadership development, building local trust by co-designing projects with local players and by generating chains of local joint success/actions rather than solving the entire issue at once. This way small solutions can be replicated rapidly, to get the action where the opportunities are.

The first section of this chapter describes a broader trend of bottom-up initiatives. In the next section, the specific developments of social innovation, which were sparked from the Resilience Action Initiative, are described. Finally, I give a perspective on how corporates can use bottom-up innovation to create a competitive advantage, while also touching upon some of the key intrinsic challenges of bottom-up innovation.

Fading boundaries and stronger horizontal and local networks

Young people are less reliant on traditional institutions like governments, NGOs, corporates or political parties to create impact. This could be witnessed with the Arab Spring and the Occupy Wall Street movement. Bottom-up initiatives develop against a backdrop of increased responsibility, fading corporate boundaries and stronger horizontal and local networks.

> We are becoming increasingly aware that solutions to our global challenges must purposefully engage youth, at all levels – locally, regionally, nationally and globally. This generation has the passion, dynamism and entrepreneurial spirit to shape the future.
> – *Professor Klaus Schwab, World Economic Forum Founder and Executive Chairman*

Several factors have led to an increased sense of responsibility from people within existing institutions, and in particular corporates, to act for the better and improve the state of the world. These are the visibility of negative effects of the way we manage resources; the increased empowerment mainly driven by financial independence for individuals to react to this and mobilise their peers via social network sites to protest against existing policies and institutions; as well as the inability of existing institutions to address these challenges alone.

> If we all act together, business, governments, NGOs and citizens – and especially the young – just imagine the good we could create. We not only need the help the young can give us but their enthusiasm, ambition, drive and ideas, too. Today over half the world's population is under 30. [...] There is a new, more entrepreneurial spirit among today's young people. Young people have the opportunity, the responsibility and duty to be the catalysts for change. They all have the potential to be leaders and changemakers.
>
> – *Paul Polman, CEO Unilever*

CEOs like Paul Polman of Unilever are front-runners in showing what is possible – and show that these changes can go hand-in-hand with direct business interests. At all levels individuals are responding. Within corporates social intrapreneurship is the new buzzword – intrapreneurs are people who act as social changemakers from within existing corporates.

At the same time, corporate boundaries are fading. Challenges are increasingly interconnected. By solving an energy shortage, a water shortage can be created – because most forms of energy production require water. When producing 'clean energy' from biofuels, large amounts of arable land have to be planted with energy crops – land which otherwise could have been used to produce food. Therefore, companies can take a competitive advantage when they operate across their traditional vertical boundaries. Shell is growing reed beds in Oman to green the desert, using wastewater from its oilfield operations. Utilities in Europe and the USA develop apps for their customers to be able to bring down their energy demand. Coca-Cola invests in ecosystem restoration to improve water catchment in areas where they bottle their drinks.

An important driver for bottom-up innovation is the development of stronger horizontal and local networks. Most of these networks are enabled through the Internet. The demonstrations at Tahrir Square in Cairo were not organised by one single leader, but by the local community as a whole. And they were supported by the global community – through social media. These events showed the world that many small initiatives, organised by individuals who feel responsible and act across traditional institutional boundaries, can have a tremendous impact – and are very difficult to manage from within the traditional response framework.

How to engage with a movement, when you don't know whom their spokesperson is?

Local and horizontal networks create an entirely new way of doing business with a focus on sharing rather than having. A prime example is Airbnb, which is becoming a threat to the hotel industry by offering low-price accommodation within large cities by people renting out their own home.[3] Also car sharing is becoming increasingly popular.[4] The sharing economy is based on local and horizontal networks, operating in the absence of large head offices and associated vertical structures, based on trust between individuals. In this world it doesn't matter which company you work for and which title is on your business card – it matters what you do with it.

Against these trends, the development of bottom-up initiatives to increase resilience is a natural phenomenon. It sparks from the increased sense of responsibility of employees working for large corporates, who feel their *own* responsibility to make their local communities more resilient to energy-water-food stress. It also sparks from the interconnectedness of these challenges and the realisation that it is impossible to tackle these challenges in isolation. Lastly, the existing horizontal networks support informal local collaboration to address these challenges in unconventional, bottom-up structures.

What would a world look like if networked, horizontal, local initiatives become the standard rather than the exception? If individuals take more responsibility for their environment? If corporate boundaries are fading such that a person's skills and expertise for a certain job become more important than their rank or seniority?

This is a world in which corporates (and governments) are structures along which knowledge, resources and networks are shared and in which society's challenges are addressed. Every company and every country is managed through the lens of social enterprise – aiming to minimise the costs of social and environmental externalities, and to have a net positive impact. There are billions of self-employed, highly skilled and flexible workers, who deliver on a demand basis, locally embedded but globally connected. A sense of meaning and trust-based relationships, more than a sense of status and financial reward for performance, will attract the

---

3   Airbnb has served 9 million guests since it was founded 5 years ago (in 2009), and has doubled the number of guests from 2012 to 2013. Techcrunch.com

4   The number of carsharing members in the US and Europe has grown from 1 million in 2009 to 3 million in 2012 and is expected to grow to 10 million in 2016 (Rocky Mountain Institute [2010]).

highest talent to deliver a certain job. Talent will search for the most challenging issues, with the highest societal relevance (meaning a positive environmental and social impact). They will seek institutions that stand out as taking the responsibility to act – because there they find a match with their values. The millennials leverage their own networks. All they need is space and the freedom to decide how best to spend their time, with whom to connect and where to do work.[5]

The bottom-up perspective significantly challenges existing corporate business models. It requires a shift from upscaling towards downscaling: rather than looking for a country-wide solution to address all challenges at once, start small and replicate successful approaches quickly. It needs a shift from short-term thinking to meet this quarter's targets to longer term thinking to serve the consumer's needs 20 years on. It also needs a shifting perspective: rather than looking forward, looking around. What solutions and opportunities are already available? But most of all it needs a shift in the way the company is managed. Creating space for social innovation means creating time for employees to work on this, making this an integral part of their job. This implies creating the right incentives, as well as a high level of trust.

Initial results

Under the Resilience Action Initiative, a programme of bottom-up innovations has been rolled out in multiple locations. In the programme, Shell young professionals mobilise their peers from other multinationals, NGOs and city government as well as local entrepreneurs. Together they make a plan to increase the resilience of the community in which they are living and working, and realise it. The approach is highly action-oriented. The projects need to have tangible results within one year, results that you can touch and feel, while at the same time they need to have a sustainable and scalable business case.

The teams design their own urban projects from scratch, based on the demand from the city and their most critical issues with respect to the nexus, their own capabilities and the passions of the individual team members.

Pilots are run by local project leaders on a voluntary basis. They chair a cross-functional team with other young professionals from different companies and government/civil society to run the projects. Funding require-

5   PwC, University of Southern California and London Business School (2013)

ments are small in the first year (€5 to €50k per project) – funding is the responsibility of local project teams and can be organised from companies, government and/or other investors. Once the projects achieve scale, they can lead to start-ups or can be incorporated in existing businesses.

A central programme manager provides support to local project team leaders. This support involves a link to strategy, knowledge on resilience/nexus and process such as how to manage a bottom-up project. The programme manager facilitates peer-to-peer connections and knowledge sharing between different projects worldwide.

Example: Edible walls

Young professionals from Shell, Yara, McKinsey & Co and IBM helped schools to build 'edible walls' to make children aware of their own role in local sustainable food production and to make them see the connection between food production and use of energy and water.

Innovative?

On 27 September 2013, 20 children from Rotterdam opened an edible wall at the Klimop school in the north of Rotterdam. Since then, kids at the Klimop can eat from the walls of their school.

"Everywhere around the world you find vertical gardens, but producing food verti-cally is still unexisting. Except for now, at these two schools in Rotterdam", says Charlie Minter, local project leader from the National Thinktank. "We should be proud of this!"

Getting started

The schools were happy to collaborate on this initiative. Kids design and plant their own vertical vegetable and fruit garden with strawberries, herbs and berries. They learn to take care of the wall and the crops, how to prune and harvest, and thereby they become more aware of how fruit and vegetables are being produced.

Thekla Teunis from Shell explains: "With this project we want to make children and young professionals aware of the fact that they can contribute to increasing the resilience of the food supply chain, with a tangible local project. To realise this initia-tive, Shell worked together with young professionals from Yara, McKinsey & Co., IBM, Stichting Move, the National Thinktank, the Rotterdam Climate Initiative and STEK urban garden shop in Rotterdam. All organisations care about making children and young professionals aware of their own role in local and resilient food production. The interlinkages between energy, water and food production play an important role in the project. Edible vertical walls are water-efficient and you need less energy to get the food on your plate than when you transport it from the other side of the world."

The founders of the initiative are seeking to expand it to other schools, individuals and public spaces in the city. To be able to expand the initiative, the costs need to be reduced. Therefore the team is working on developing a low-cost system for the walls. The final ambition is to make vertical urban gardens and food production in large cities worldwide possible.

The following criteria were defined to determine what constitutes a successful bottom-up project under the Resilience Action Initiative:
- The project contributes to increased resilience in terms of energy-water-food issues.
- The project is tangible and doable: it is designed and executed by young professionals from within multinationals, linked with local entrepreneurs.
- The business model is replicable.
- It leads to a spinoff business and/or is incorporated in a government or multinational. The participating institutions are seed funders/shareholders in the initiative locally.
- It is a collaborative effort; preferably there is a mix between public and private sector investors.
- The young professionals consider their experience in the project useful and indicate they have learnt new ways of collaborating across the fence line.

The objective is to generate sustainable and scalable business models. This is done by developing a funnel of ideas through a stage-gated type of funnel. The project coordinators receive a step-by-step guide to managing the team through this process.

Project generation funnel

	Long list of project ideas	Shortlist of top 5 ideas	Feasible ideas; interest from companies	Ideas with business case	Funded pilot projects	Spinoffs into real business
Phase	Kickoff	Kickoff	Validation	Business case	Execution	Scaling
Time	½ day	½ day	1 month	3-4 months	3-4 months	...

After the small but inspiring project in Rotterdam, young professionals started similar initiatives in other locations.

In South Africa, concrete project ideas were developed for designing more resilient housing, creating a movie to raise awareness around energy, water and food stress and a creating a market where farmers can not only exchange products but also knowledge on sustainable farming practices.

One of the projects is being executed. It focuses on collaborative business models for restoration of degraded land. Around 20% of the world's ecosystems are threatened and this situation is worsening with an alarming speed. Healthy ecosystems are critical to increase the resilience of local communities, and ecosystem services like agriculture, carbon capture and water are highly valuable for businesses as well as government. The good news is that this degradation can be reversed by actively restoring landscapes.

This pilot aims to make the match between the local business community (including the young professionals from the RAI companies) and an existing initiative on ecosystem restoration in South Africa. The purpose of the project is to actively create an innovative sustainable business case for ecosystem restoration and sustainable agriculture in the area, in partnership with the academic, NGO and business communities, and to explore the potential for collaboration in other areas.

Key to the approach is to start creating action on the ground and learn from what has already been done locally. If successful, the approach can be scaled and rolled out to many other areas in which the participating companies have critical business interests.

In Groningen in the Netherlands, young professionals from Shell are working with a team made up of all kinds of backgrounds and industries. The project focuses on consumer energy efficiency for disadvantaged communities, energy-efficient lighting and reducing food waste. Existing food box initiatives, supplying organic food on a weekly basis to customers, will be linked to available food waste in the city. The project team has identified new customers segments for these boxes in socially disadvantaged communities, but also via employees of the corporates. The leaders of the initiative state: "We set up this initiative after an inspiring story from our colleagues in Rotterdam, on stage during the Shell Ecomarathon. The idea that they had been able to achieve tangible results within one year to actually increase the resilience of Rotterdam in a collaborative effort inspired us to set up a similar initiative here. The experience has contributed to our leadership skills in the following ways:

- Contact with a very diverse group of stakeholders from the city where we live and work.
- Having a broad perspective for tackling complex issues and creating connections between existing initiatives.
- Generating enthusiasm and supporting a group of young professionals with a wide variety of backgrounds and interests."

The ultimate goal of this programme will be to build a movement of change-makers. The ambition is to scale up to 50 successful projects in 2016. In one location, several projects can run in parallel. To strengthen the collaborative character of the initiative, young professionals from other multinationals are invited to become project managers as well.

Main lessons

What went well
Young professionals in corporations respond with great energy to being given the opportunity to create and execute innovative ideas. Selecting people on enthusiasm, and empowering them to get on with the job, accelerates the process and deepens motivation. Basic project management competence always matters, including being clear about timelines, responsibility and deliverables. External stakeholders, in this case from the city administration, were involved from the very beginning and the team worked with others with diverse perspectives, such as impact investors.

Barriers to overcome
Inevitably there was a large attrition rate amongst projects, with about one in five projects making it from kickoff to realisation. This was due to a wide range of causes, including lack of support from the line managers, poorly articulated goals, inability to attract funding or simply not enough time and energy. The most promising initiatives were chaired by the project leaders themselves, with a strong commitment to achieving impact.

A few recommendations
Addressing differences in company culture and way of working upfront during one of the first meetings helps. Seed funding is always a challenge for entrepreneurs, but in this case arranging some funding upfront from existing budgets within the corporates helps. These funds can be used as matching funds to accelerate piloting of potentially successful ideas. Only

€5,000 to €10,000 was typically needed for this to be effective. Support is essential, since typically young professionals have little experience with local entrepreneurship and need some support to find their way in a city. An experienced facilitator and social entrepreneur can help the teams to remain focused and push for implementation. Finally support from line managers and senior management is critical to give employees the feeling that they are rewarded for their efforts. Innovation, so also bottom-up innovation, comes with failure. It is critical to acknowledge this and to actively applaud risk-taking by the employees.

> I don't see myself working for any organisation and climbing the corporate ca-
> reer ladder. I just want to develop my own talents as much as possible, and do the
> best I can to make the world a better place. I will organise my own work – I trust
> that will work.
> – *Member of the Global Shapers community of the World Economic Forum,*
> *Amsterdam*

Barriers for breakthrough bottom-up innovation

For bottom-up initiatives to be successful and have impact, traditional business scaling is not the way to go, it is replication. It is about copying small successes, rather than scaling them. There's a subtle difference in that. Rather than having one big multinational company building edible walls, the goal is to create several hubs connected in a networked organisation or cooperation, which deliver edible walls worldwide – in their own way and matching local needs. However, if replicability is a key criterion, it means impact is determined by the replication speed, or in network terms the contagion rate.

To increase the contagion rate, an innovation should be sustainable, size-able and self-organised.[6] *Sustainable* means it might need some funding to get started, but once they passed pilot stage the services or products can sustain themselves without continuous public hand-outs or having to go to cap-in-hand foundations and donors,[7] including the corporates. The fund-seeking activities take time and they limit flexibility. *Sizeable* means the innovations "are designed from scratch to scale". So they apply at a very local level and an individual school like the edible walls, but they can reach millions of custom-

6   Jankel (2011)
7   Ibidem

ers living in large cities with vertical surfaces worldwide. The last criterion is that the innovation needs to be *self-organised*. This means it "leverages the capacity of grassroots, decentralised, localised and in-culture individuals and communities to co-create and co-deliver the services themselves".[8] For the edible walls, this would mean a toolkit developing through which every single individual can build an edible wall using local products themselves.

Business value

Bottom-up innovation provides the opportunity for corporates to engage in new ways of collaborating. It provides an opportunity to broaden the funnel of future investment opportunities. It can be a low-key step-up towards building trust-based relationships with key stakeholders in country. It provides an opportunity to develop the most talented young professionals and let them experience first-hand new ways of working together with different players in society. All of this will lead to increased resilience locally.

It is impossible to solve all nexus issues at once, but if we start building a chain of local actions, we can trigger a movement of change. A small-scale approach will allow rapid scaling, to get the action where the opportunities and 'demand' are. Collaboration is about trust, and trust is about relationships between people, at an individual level. In the projects, strong focus is put on building local trust by co-designing projects with local players at a small scale and by generating small success quickly. A joint success will increase the level of trust between the participants. The project is designed from scratch by the participants to ensure ownership and responsibility for the end result and increase local impact. Senior stakeholders are asked to set the project boundaries, but not determine the shape and form of the project itself. The projects like the edible walls are small and in an experimental stage, but if successful, they can be rolled out rapidly all over the world, using the global outreach of the corporates involved.

It is in the enlightened self-interest of the corporate world to enable young talent to generate actions connecting with local communities everywhere, to build local trust and increase resilience of local systems – and corporate structures as well.

> Happiness is to discover the brilliant possibilities of the hidden change in the world.
> – *Alain Badiou*

8   Ibidem

9   Corporations and Resilience

Simone Arizzi,[1] Maximilian Egger,[2] Dawn Rittenhouse[3] and Peter Williams[4]

The Resilience Action Initiative

The Resilience Action Initiative (RAI) described in this book is not only unique for the resilience approach it took to address pervasive stresses at the water-energy-food nexus, but also for the broad and diverse set of competencies, capabilities and cultures the different participating companies brought to bear on the issue. In this chapter we take a look at the RAI experience over the past two years as a global collaborative effort among private sector partners, attempting to derive some broader lessons from the experience. We hope that what we learned in this period – among private sector companies only – might also extend to the public-private partnerships that will ultimately be required to solve resilience challenges at the energy, food and water nexus.

When the initiative started in 2012, resilience was a relatively novel concept for large private sector companies. The genuine interest in joining forces and developing a set of new tools and collaborative business models that could contribute to the systemic resilience of cities, regions and countries rapidly evolved into a discussion on the best approach. Should we develop a set of general recommendations and best practices based on the individual or collective experience of some of the member companies having faced similar challenges? Or should we be focusing on a set of real situations where the power of the collaborative approach could be applied and validated in its capability to improve the resilience of that specific system? This later approach was chosen, defining from the very beginning a key characteristic of the initiative which is to learn by doing, demonstrating the impact of the collaborative approach on specific pilot projects. As described in Chapter 1, a pilot project is focused on a city, industrial setting or other geographic location where the companies might test a resilience approach, collaborating with local authorities and stakeholders,

1   Technology & Innovation Director, EMEA, at DuPont
2   Senior Consultant, Energy Sector, Siemens
3   Director Sustainability for the DuPont Company
4   Chief Technology Officer, Big Green Innovations, at IBM, and an IBM Distinguished Engineer

to minimise system stresses at the water-energy-food nexus. This approach has several advantages:

- It is focused. The geographic location is clearly defined, simplifying both the identification of the challenges and the quantification of the impact of the collaborative approach.
- It is inclusive. Participation in a pilot project is voluntary, driven by the willingness to contribute competencies and technologies toward the solution of those specific resilience issues in which each member has the most experience.
- It can be used again. All pilot projects target real-world situations where the lessons from each project can be applied to similar settings in other parts of the world, making future iterations simpler and faster in their implementation.

In the period 2012-2013 about a dozen pilot projects were proposed and assessed within the RAI framework across all regions. Below we distill what worked well and what could have been done better:

Lesson 1. Collaborative behaviour and a diversity of skills are essential
RAI was designed to include companies from across many sectors, in order to have a diversity of skills and competences to apply.

One specific example comes from the collaborative efforts in Da Nang in Vietnam where, in a precursor project to RAI, IBM and Shell representatives worked together to address water management and transportation issues for the city government. The combination of Shell's civil, mechanical and production engineering skills (and habits of mind) with IBM's information systems engineering skills and thought processes proved constructive.

Lesson 2. Combine thinking and doing
The primary focus of RAI was on action in the form of projects on the ground. However, it was clear from the start that developing a shared and tested methodology would be essential to looking through a resilience lens, contributing to creating a shared language and ultimately making clear choices. With the engagement of all RAI members, significant effort was put in providing practical guidance to each pilot using prior experiences. In turn the progress of each pilot also offered opportunities drawn from real situations to further refine the originally established methodology. The time it takes to develop a new shared frame should not be underestimated, and although there is much literature on resilience, transposing it so that it is helpful in a corporate context takes substantial effort and investment.

Lesson 3. Business cannot do this alone

RAI was originally created as a private sector initiative in order to share and build a corporate perspective. However it became progressively clearer during the implementation phase of the individual pilots that resilience has to be tackled in a partnership between public and private sectors – neither side can 'go it alone' as neither has all the resources, connections and insights needed. As the maker of policy, the public sector has a broad role and impact. For example its policies influence land use practice, define public infrastructure, and its convening power is often needed to engage and align stakeholders. The private sector can contribute its skills, project management capacity, a different way of framing the issues, and sophisticated supply chains. The importance of cross sector collaboration has of course been emphasised elsewhere. For a more resilient outcome to come about, it is a necessary but not sufficient condition.

Collaboration is an imperative, but it alone does not guarantee a resilience approach. Not only must there be collaboration between sectors, there must also be a joint application of the resilience lens to come up with the kind of innovative and adaptive solutions that will meet the challenge.

This was also in evidence on Singapore's Jurong Island where several RAI partners joined forces to investigate how the energy efficiency of such an industrial cluster might be improved. In particular, the sharing of steam among tenants may hold the potential to contribute to the resilience of Singapore by further reducing dependence on imported fuels and underpinning the competitiveness of the cluster. While doing the assessment was a big effort, realising the benefit could not occur without deep engagement of the authorities, to look at adapting the rules and regulations for this to occur.

Lesson 4. Resilience is relevant to many corporate functions, but does not yet have a natural "home"

RAI was initiated by the CEOs of the companies, but finding an organisational home for operationalising the initiative was not obvious. Some companies delegated it to sustainability officers, others to strategy, technology, regulatory, corporate strategy or communication staff. Resilience being a relatively new concept for most private companies it is certainly not surprising that its home, if it even exists, is assigned across many corporate functions.

Mirroring the debates on the organisational home of sustainability a decade ago, there is no obvious right answer. The Rockefeller Foundation's 100 Resilient Cities initiative resolves this issue for cities by providing funding for dedicated chief resilience officers in the participating cities.

These can then act as catalysts for resilience thinking, which hopefully over time becomes integrated into the organisation. For the RAI companies, defining the organisational anchors for resilience is very much work in progress, and will require different solutions depending on the respective organisational structure and culture. Whichever organisational home is found for resilience, there is also a risk that without collaboration across the organisation such an approach may also confine resilience to its own organisational 'ghetto' with no real influence over day-to-day activities.

Lesson 5. Traditional business metrics do not capture resilience
Businesses like metrics. They help focus and measure progress. However as we've seen in previous chapters, resilience is not easily captured in simple metrics, particularly as the desirable level of resilience should vary with time and context. In some cases a purposeful decrease in resilience may be necessary, such as when change is needed and rigid structures should be dismantled to allow for renewal. Advisors to RAI guarded against an early and hurried adoption of metrics, as potentially being counter productive. Still, the lack of clear resilience metrics is a problem for businesses, who need metrics to focus management and effort. The challenge in establishing clear resilience metrics then translate in a difficulty for businesses in engaging on the topic at the operational level.

The tools described in Chapters 2 and 3 will lead to identifying solutions and actions to address the resilience of the particular system under consideration. Once a project is defined, one may revert to more traditional metrics to drive to results. Too narrow a focus on those results holds the danger that the project misses its target, as interactions and external factors may well require adjustment. For example, Chapter 6 describes the challenge of realising and scaling 'green' infrastructure projects, as these require more adaptation to an evolving context than the 'grey' infrastructure projects they aim to replace.

Businesses need to be aware that traditional metrics do not capture resilience, and that a set of appropriate metrics for it will evolve naturally over time, based on a more sophisticated appreciation of risk and mitigation. However by applying the appropriate resilience tools, the required practical project priorities can still be set.

Lesson 6. Companies struggle to take the required long-term perspective
Private companies are constantly under pressure to deliver short-term performance, while keeping an eye on the long term. Both direct risks to themselves, and the broader risks of losing alignment with the concerns

of society should worry them. The resilience lens helps to shine a light on both these threats. With some notable exceptions, the private sector has a tendency to ignore risks that it finds too uncomfortable, at least until some event forces an even more uncomfortable confrontation with reality. That is however starting to change. The SEC now requires publicly listed companies to report material environmental risks; the 2010 flooding in Thailand seems to have had a salutary impact in showing what can happen, especially to JIT supply chains that have been denuded of buffer stocks in the interests of efficiency; and the compilations of data from the insurance industry, EM-DAT and others, showing the trend in natural disasters are also having an impact. RAI itself is an example of companies engaging with the longer-term issues of society and how they can add value by providing new types of solutions.

Lesson 7. Financing resilience requires new business models
The benefits and costs of resilience actions accrue in different patterns over time – and to different stakeholders. This makes financing more resilient solutions difficult. It is perhaps a truism that governments' propensity to invest seems to be directly related to how recent and how severe the last extreme event was. To a certain extent this is true of companies as well. When looking to increase the resilience of socio-economic systems, all these challenges are compounded: It requires a longer-term perspective, it requires a way of considering risk distributions that do not follow normal patterns as described in Chapter 3 and it requires a way to transfer value over time. These challenges have no simple solutions, but acknowledging them and making them an element of collaboration for resilience is helpful.

Companies themselves can act by expanding their risk management frames, as some are already doing with the advent of supply chain problems. The Center for Resilience at Ohio State University is one example where tools are being developed to help companies execute this better.[5]

It became clear in several pilot projects that addressing resilience will require new business models and in particular new financing approaches that help address these shifting benefits and costs.

Lesson 8. Resilience requires a systemic perspective – and that is not easy for the modern business organisation
During RAI implementation work it was apparent that people from various walks of life – once introduced to the resilience topic – would readily see

5   Fiksel (2010)

the negative consequences of its absence and would spot different effects depending on their background or aspects important to their situation. On the other hand it is much harder to act for the prevention of the negative impacts of unforeseen, unusual or unscheduled events.

Much of the difficulty stems from the fact that resilience requires taking a systemic perspective. Companies are often successful because they have perfected the art of adequately resolving a specific and difficult problem in a consistent and predictable fashion, treating it in relative isolation. Yet taking into account all the factors that can influence the problem, and collaboratively delivering solutions that are also adaptable over time, is a very big change, both in capability and also in mindset. Resilience will require a stronger capacity to recognise the impact of the broader systems perspective.

Conclusion

In this chapter we have described some lessons that we offer to future actors and stakeholders who will work in the implementation of resilience approaches to mitigate various stresses. By and large these were the result of hands-on experimentation carried out by motivated individuals from about a dozen multinational companies over two years, in the form of pilot projects.

For companies themselves, resilience must be a matter for shareholders, supervisory boards and top management. It is the chairmen and chair-women, the CEOs and the CFOs together with shareholder representatives who must all take a resilience lens, to look into the future of the companies they are responsible for. As we've seen, this requires familiarity with the new lens of resilience, the adoption of new tools and an expansion of risk management frameworks. Doing so will not only be helpful to the companies, but will also be the platform for being able to engage with customers and stakeholders to address societal resilience issues. Companies that adopt a resilience lens internally, will not only be doing their fiduciary duty of safeguarding the companies' interests, but they will also be more attuned to emerging societal and customer needs and opportunities.

Our world has become complex, multi-faceted, globalised, fast as well as interdependent. Manufacturing and trade, education and prosperity, finance and administration, politics and business, urbanisation and en-vironment, welfare and demographic change, and another endless list of aspects bind us together or make us struggle with each other across the globe like never before in history. It is clear that increasingly we face similar problems. It is also obvious that one can't solve these challenges alone. This complexity needs an equally sophisticated approach to solutions – a common approach.

Therefore – and again, we refer to the extreme events of recent years – and to the experiences during our RAI implementation work – to strongly advocate more collaboration and joint action of private and public stakeholders. Company owners and managers and state and local government officials need to form a new joint vision and implement coordinated resilience strategies to safeguard welfare and prosperity in the face of the energy-water-food nexus.

What our experience has shown is that implementing resilience also requires openness to novel formats of collaboration for solutions to be successful. In the future we may well first see working platforms that evolve on bilateral or local level. National awareness, regulation and facilitation could come from heads of state and business leaders, ministerial offices and business associations. In its magnitude and quality what we advocate may well represent a new era of broader collective action between private and public stakeholders, and make a significant contribution to prosperity for a growing world population.

Epilogue

Brian Walker[1]

The Resilience Action Initiative is an example from the corporate world of developing an adaptive approach to a difficult complex systems problem. It does not adopt a fixed policy approach; it assumes that learning by doing is necessary and that policies and management must change. It is therefore very much in line with resilience thinking and – for those involved in developing resilience ideas and theory – it is a very welcome initiative. What kinds of things does a 'resilience approach' call for? The best way to answer this is with an example, and so I'll start by using one with which I'm familiar. But first let me be clear about how resilience is defined and used by scientists, because it differs somewhat from those used by practitioners earlier in this book. The formal definition is "the capacity to absorb disturbance and reorganise so as to retain essentially the same *function*, *structure* and feedbacks – to have the same *identity*". More informally, a usable definition is "the ability to cope with shocks and to keep functioning in much the same kind of way".

The example I'll use to illustrate a resilience approach is how best to use the resources in the Murray-Darling Basin (MDB), Australia's most important agricultural region. With 60,000 farms, 15,000 of them using irrigation, lots of towns and villages and three big rivers flowing through four states, the MDB is a self-organising, social-ecological system that functions at multiple scales, with strong connections and feedback effects across scales.

In its early development, before a proper assessment of the river flows had been made, water rights were over-allocated, and now in drier years there simply isn't enough water to allocate farmers' full rights; and if those water off-take levels were to continue the rivers and their floodplains would die.

This led the states and the federal government to form the Murray Darling Basin Commission, to manage the water and determine how much 'environmental water' should be taken back. It produced a 'plan' that unfortunately dealt separately with environmental and socio-economic issues. The commission was then replaced by a new MDB Authority (MDBA), which has produced a revised Basin Plan, now accepted by the states and the federal government, addressing how best to achieve necessary levels of diversion of water from irrigation back to the environment. It considers

1   Chairman, The Resilience Alliance

the environmental, social and economic interactions arising from proposed changes in water allocations, in a resilience context. The approach it is adopting is a work-in-progress, but involves the following:

It begins with developing an agreed, explicit description - a 'conceptual model' - of the 'system'. This is not trivial, because different players and stakeholders have very different understandings of what is really important, what is 'in' and 'out' of the system, how it works, and what is really important.

Developing such an explicit mental model emphasises things that are often ignored or not appreciated, like who are the key players/stakeholders? What are the critical scales at which the system functions? What time scales are important to everyone? What do people value – the resilience of what? Working through this develops an awareness of issues such as:

– You cannot understand or manage the system at one scale; a common mistake. Like all complex systems, the MDB is a multi-scale, linked social-ecological system and the connections across scales are mostly what cause both social and ecological problems. Everyone needs to appreciate this.

– Resilience, per se, is neither 'good' nor 'bad'. Undesirable states of systems can be very resilient (dictatorships, saline landscapes). Sometimes it's necessary to reduce resilience, in order to effect a positive change.

– Making a system very resilient in one way can cause it to lose resilience in other ways, at other scales; there is often a trade-off in managing for resilience.

– The 'rule of hand': At any one scale there are no more than three to five critical controlling variables – the things that really matter.

As the evolving description of the system proceeds (there will never be a final, complete version), three components of resilience are considered. They are presented briefly below, but a fuller account is given in Walker and Salt (2012):

1. The existence of thresholds (discontinuities) in the behaviour of a system.
2. The capacity to deal with disturbances and to manage and change, or to avoid, thresholds. This is known as adaptive capacity, or general resilience.
3. Transformation capacity – the capacity to transform parts of the system into a different kind of system when continuation of the existing one is no longer possible.

I'll briefly consider each in turn:

1. Thresholds. Two solutions to the over-allocation of water problem are being pursued – buying back water, and becoming more efficient in using it, including reducing losses in canals, and so forth. Putting a resilience lens over this introduces a focus on thresholds. Are there any known or likely discontinuities in regard to levels/supplies of water that would have significant consequences, either ecologically or socio-economically?

For example, if a river needs a minimum of X giga-litres of flow for it to retain its biodiversity and avoid becoming eutrophic, there's little point in buying back water that achieves less than X. That is so obvious that people are already working on it. But there are many other kinds of thresholds that are not so obvious.

Some water for irrigation, and increasingly for mining, is pumped from aquifers and in some aquifers, if the amount of water drops below a critical level it results in a resorting of the aquifer bed such that its capacity to hold water is permanently reduced (so don't exceed that threshold).

And there are threshold effects in the industry part of the system. In one of the irrigation regions there used to be three dairy processing plants. As the number of dairy farms declined, milk supply dropped below a threshold for business viability and one of the plants has closed down. Threshold effects also occur in the socio-economic system, such in the debt : income ratio, and in levels of labour supply, so thresholds need to be considered in all aspects of the dynamics of complex systems.

A resilience approach, therefore, asks the question: "What and where are possible thresholds?" and "What feedback processes are involved?"

How to go about answering this is a large topic, but in essence it involves a focus on the controlling feedback processes that determine the self-organising dynamics. Negative feedbacks have a dampening effect and positive feedbacks amplify any changes. Studies of resilience repeatedly show that thresholds occur where there is a significant change in an important feedback. It can be a change from being small to big, or negative to positive, as critical parts of the system change. In the MDB the feedback changes that have caused most problems have been those between the biophysical and the socio-economic parts of the system; a change in the agro-ecological part of the system leads to a change in the behaviour of people, often elsewhere in the system, and their changed actions then feed back to further changes in the agro-ecological part, and so forth.

In working with catchment managers I have found that a useful way of getting engaged has been through developing what are called 'state-and-transition' (S&T) models; conceptual models that describe the possible states the system can be in (fertile soil vs salinised; floodplains with healthy regenerating redgums vs without redgums), etc. It starts by asking "What state is the system in now?" and then, "What other possible states could it be in?" Then, for each possible transition between pairs of states, ask the question "Are there any likely thresholds? If so, what is causing them – what feedbacks are involved?" These simple conceptual S&T models can be developed further into quantitative, analytical models for thresholds that are clearly important.

2. *Adaptive capacity* (managing and avoiding thresholds). Attributes that contribute to resilience, in general, that have thus far emerged from resilience analyses in various parts of the world include:
– High functional diversity – units/groups/species that perform different, complementary functions that together keep the whole system function-ing well.
– High response diversity – different units/species that perform the same function but in different ways, or at different scales. This warns against blind pursuit of increasing efficiency by removing what are perceived as redundancies.
– Being modular in structure – avoiding the dangers of over-connectedness (rapid transmission of diseases, malfunctions), and of lack of connections.
– Having tight feedbacks – being able to detect and respond quickly to changes as their effects feed back to other parts of the system.
– Being 'open' – allowing and enabling movement (i.e. emigration and immigration).
– Having reserves – biophysical (like seed banks in ecosystems), financial and social (like memory).
– Fostering innovation, novelty and continuous learning.
– High social capital – especially trust, leadership, social networks.
– Equality/equity – high inequity is associated with a range of negative, costly social features (prison rates, obesity, teenage births, etc.) that together lower response capacity and resilience.[2]
– Adaptive governance – especially overlapping institutions and polycen-tric governance, and flexible distributive governance.

I conclude this emerging list of attributes with a comment on an important misconception about resilience: It is *not* about not changing. Trying to

2   Wilkinson and Pickett (2010)

prevent disturbance and keep a system constant reduces its resilience. A forest in which fire is always prevented eventually loses the species capable of withstanding fire; the only way for a forest to remain resilient to fire is for it to be burned every now and then. Probing the boundaries of resilience is necessary for maintaining and building resilience.

To help in thinking through these resilience attributes, and which of them might be important, it is useful to do it in parallel with the attempts to develop the set of possible threshold effects.

3. *Transformation.* Transformation and resilience are not opposites; they work together across scales. For the MDB to continue into the future as an agricultural system delivering high levels of human wellbeing, not all the parts of it can continue doing what they are doing now. Some parts of the Basin will have to transform. Some farms will have to change from being irrigation farms to some other kind of enterprise.

Transformability, the capacity to transform, involves three steps: First, getting beyond the state of denial (people hate fundamental change, and they resist it – sometimes until it is too late for other options). Second, identifying and creating new options, new trajectories for the system. This puts a focus on experiments and novelty, trying new things knowing that many will fail, and it emphasises the need for the next step. Third, developing the capacity to change, which depends on the levels of all the five capitals (natural, human, social, built and financial) and, *especially*, on governance and support from higher levels (like government). My experience with regional groups attempting to undergo real change suggests that under the difficult conditions when transformation is called for, government assistance is very often in the form of help *not to* change, rather than help *to* change. Transformation failure seems mostly due to inappropriate or poor governance.

Conclusion

I conclude with an evolving set of lessons about how to build resilience, and an observation.

The lessons
- Don't try to aim for some 'optimal' state; learn to ride the system piggy-back ('guided self-organisation', adaptive management and governance)
- Learn about thresholds, to avoid unwanted states

- Restrict control of environmental/ecological variability
- Identify the main scales at which the system functions
- Think about feedbacks and secondary effects, especially cross-scale and cross-domain (beware of partial solutions!)
- Maintain general resilience and embrace change
- Promote and sustain diversity, of all kinds (don't confuse 'redundancy' and 'response diversity')
- Encourage learning, innovation and experiments
- Be ready for and capable of transformational change

An observation

In confronting the question "How might the corporate world engage with resilience?", most businesses will ask: what's in it for us? And the problem is that when adopting a resilience approach acts against the immediate interests of the business, denial sets in; as summed up nicely in the well-known quote: It is very hard to get someone to understand something when his salary depends on him not understanding it.

A single company focused on its own success is unlikely to contribute significantly to the resilience of the whole system in which it functions; the business world is too competitive. And hence the value of the RAI, as the harbinger of a shift in the philosophy of corporate development. If major business groups in the world, covering the spectrum of their resource activities (as both sources and sinks), could assess and then act to enhance the resilience of their collective environment and hence the resilience of their own collective system, they would greatly contribute to sustainability – not just of their set of companies, but of the world in general.

Appendix

GREEN INFRASTRUCTURE CASE STUDIES

Case Studies evaluated by participating companies for the creation of the White Paper *The Case for Green Infrastructure*

JUNE 2013

Table of Contents

Dow: phytoremediation for groundwater decontamination

Source/organisation: The Dow
Chemical Company

Scale: Large – Dow Sarnia installation is
roughly 2 acres with 1,300 trees within
the fence line of the chemical complex
site which is no longer in operation

Key stakeholder(s): Dow/regulatory
body

Project phase: Fully implemented for
2 years

Geographical location: Sarnia, Ontario, Canada

Sarnia Site, the Dow Chemical Company

PROJECT OVERVIEW

Phytoremediation is the engineered use of green plants to remove, contain,
stabilise or destroy contaminants in the soil and groundwater. The uptake of
groundwater by the plants can achieve containment of the groundwater and
contamination (tree is basically acting as a solar pump). Engineered planted
systems can degrade, extract and control the groundwater contamination. Dow has several field pilot demonstration projects in place and fully
operational projects using phytoremediation to draw experience from.

One specific installation was completed at the Dow Sarnia facility. This
large industrial complex contained several manufacturing units that operated
for more than 60 years. The effort in ceasing operations included transitioning
the existing traditional pump and treat groundwater treatment system. The
traditional system consisted of pumping groundwater via carbon beds prior to
transferring the recovered groundwater to an external water treatment facility.

The goal of phytoremediation was to replace this existing groundwater
recovery and treatment system with a cost-effective, passive remediation
system that fully complied with environmental requirements while minimising the long-term cost of managing the site.

While still operating the pump and treat facility, the site was prepared
by minimising external infiltration and planting 1,300 trees (poplar and

willows) on an area of roughly 2 acres to handle the uptake of the ground-water. As the trees grow along with site hydrology adaptation, some of the water still needs to be pumped and treated during this transition period. This technology does require ongoing site maintenance such as sampling and analysis of ground water, hydrology testing to ensure ground water is contained, and tree management over the life of the project.

Technology maturity

Mature; a minimum of four growing seasons is necessary to prove the capability of the system. Ongoing pilot studies since 2005; Dow has over 15 sites in operation as pilots or full-scale systems.

Investment/Costs/Time

– Although the initial project cost and short-term maintenance costs for phytoremediation are significant, the NPV of the project is positive about the long-term timeline associated with this type of project.

Project management considerations

– Use of this technology depends on site characteristics, source and extent of contamination.
– Best to have pilot study since this technology is highly dependent on site-specific conditions and still considered a novel approach.
– Minimisation of long-term cost while meeting Dow and government regulations.
– Champion played an instrumental role in making this project a reality.
– Project-selection criteria: capital expenditures/ease of implementation/ease of operation/carbon footprint.
– Maximise chance of success by partnering with a consultant holding key expertise.
– Technology requires significant time to be fully operational; can be considered for non-time critical remediation projects.
– If a regulatory body is involved, need a strong and mutually respectful relationship with regulators to implement green infrastructure.
– A different technical skill set is needed to be successful with green infrastructure projects.
– Long-term project requiring multi-generational oversight.

Benefits

– No wastewater needing to be transported off site in trucks.
– No electricity required.

- Elimination of the carbon filtration system and expense related to its operation and disposal of spent carbon.
- No need for 24/7 hour operation (from an operation to a management activity).
- Significant reduction in maintenance costs compared to pump and treat.

RISKS/CHALLENGES
- Higher level of uncertainty at the onset of the project since dealing with a biological system, local geology, contaminants, site hydrology.
- Larger physical footprint than the gray alternative.
- Requires a period of growth to come to full operation.
- Try to limit interaction with biota since concerns with creating a wildlife habitat within a remediation site.
- Different set of challenges to deal with requiring different set of skills such as dealing with main disturbance (e.g. rabbits eating tree bark).
- Ensure that tight feedback and monitoring system in place to alleviate any environmental concern (e.g. leaves/pollen off the trees).

RESILIENCE ASPECTS
- Resilience is dependent on specific application, perspective and boundaries of project (How far upstream and downstream in process do you include? 'Green' and 'gray' both resist shocks, but in different ways. Gray infrastructure can be more resilient in the face of an acute stress if that stress can specifically destroy the trees; it can be rebuilt and operational in a shorter time frame. Green may be more robust in response to certain stresses such as power loss and mechanical failure.)
- Phytoremediation is multifunctional: can meet the needs of a traditional pump and treat system
- Criticality – if a quick solution has to be found – gray is the obvious choice. Green infrastructure (phytoremediation) is a longer-term option because trees take time to grow.
- Innovation – working with variety of key research bodies to increase the number of tree species being used and tested for phytoremediation potential; recognising a higher resilience in having variety of plant species.
- Modular: easy to increase capacity but still needs time to grow.
- Higher level of remediation likely over the long haul since root systems can reach everywhere – not limited to system design as in the traditional gray system.
- Traditional remediation solutions are more replicable and less site dependent.

KEY LEARNING

- The gray solution appears easier to control and manage but the long-term economic and environmental benefits of the green solution makes phytoremediation a technology that needs to be added to the portfolio of solutions when dealing with groundwater contamination.

Dow: constructed wetland for waste water treatment

Source/organisation: Union Carbide
Corporation, subsidiary of the Dow
Chemical Company

Scale: Large – 110 acres within the
fence line of Union Carbide Corporation's Seadrift Operations

Key stakeholder(s): Union Carbide
Corporation; The Dow Chemical Company; regulatory body: Texas Commission on Environmental Quality (TCEQ);
Dow 'Near neighbours' Community

Project phase: Fully operational (in
operation for 15 years)

Geographical location: North Seadrift, Texas, USA

PROJECT OVERVIEW

Seadrift is a large industrial complex containing several manufacturing units
involved in the production of plastic resins and other organic chemicals. Waste
water from the facility and storm water captured in containment areas are
routed through the wastewater treatment system. The original water treatment
system consisted of primary/secondary (anaerobic/aerobic biological) treatment ponds and a shallow tertiary pond which is approximately 267 acres with
water depth ranging from 1 to 4 feet. The tertiary pond is basically operated
as a solar stabilisation pond (no active mixing). Lower organic loads and long
detention time within the aerobic section and tertiary pond resulted in ideal
conditions for phytoplankton (floating algae bloom). This resulted in exceed-
ance of the plant's discharge permit criteria (40 mg/l) for total suspended
solids (TSS) and required extensive pH adjustments. This project was driven by
the necessity to meet EPA Effluent Guidelines for OCPSF (organic chemicals,
plastics and synthetic fibres; 40 CFR 414) facilities with regards to TSS.

Several alternative treatment options were investigated. A pilot-scale
constructed wetland project was successfully completed onsite (roughly one

year of data prior to launching the full-scale project). The conversion of part of the tertiary pond into a constructed wetland was implemented in roughly 18 months and has been in full operation since then, meeting all discharge requirements for TSS, eliminating the algal bloom issues and additionally eliminating the need to adjust discharge pH (previously done around the clock).

TECHNOLOGY MATURITY
Fully proven.

INVESTMENT/COSTS/TIME
- 1-2 year pilot study; small constructed wetland in operation in a sister plant in Mexico City.
- Fully operational 18 months after the contract was awarded.
- Initial capital investment $1.2 to $1.4 million with maintenance/operation costs dramatically reduced.

PROJECT MANAGEMENT CONSIDERATIONS
- Driver: reduce operational and maintenance cost while ensuring long-term compliance with EPA effluent guidelines (OCPSF).
- Upper management champion played an instrumental role in making this project a reality; data speaks for itself, therefore pilot study a good approach ("selling a swamp is not an easy task").
- Project selection criteria: capital expenditures/time to install/ease of implementation/ease of operation.

BENEFITS
- 100% compliant from day zero for over 15 years while eliminating the need to adjust pH.
- Low initial and operational capital required ($1.2 to 1.4 million as opposed to $40 million for gray alternative).
- Low energy and resource requirements with the corresponding environmental benefits – minimal equipment, no pumps, no additives, no oxygen system, no added water, no bio solids to handle or dispose.
- Operational support drastically different as a wetland requires minimal support from operations and maintenance, while the gray alternative requires 24/7 support.
- Construction and implementation time reduced.
- Co-benefits identified but not valued: positive impact on ecosystem (provides habitat for wildlife/educational opportunity and other soft benefits to Dow personnel and local community).

Risks/challenges

- Potential new regulations (such as coliform bacteria).
- Criteria for application of this technology: compliance with applicable regulations, water quality, salinity and large on-site physical footprint (this system would require 50 acres as opposed to 4 to 5 acres for gray alternative).
- Biotic stresses (nutria/alligators/bobcats, etc.) are the main disturbances that the system has to manage.
- There is always the potential risk that a threatened or endangered species might be found in the wetland. In the case of Seadrift, this is unlikely as none of the 46 threatened or endangered species listed by the State of Texas in the vicinity of the constructed wetland would be expected to occupy this habitat.

Resilience aspects

- Self-organising process – the wetland does not look like what was built. Now a diversified biota from plants to micro-organisms increasing the built-in stability of the mini-ecosystem to respond to fluctuations. Biodiversity is much greater in the constructed wetland than the microbiology found in conventional waste water treatment plants.
- Innovation: looking to recycle the water to attain zero discharge.
- Building understanding and management practices of ecosystems dynamics (learn to switch from operate to manage mode and to leave it alone).

Key learning

- A win in all aspects (no waste; no energy; no 24/7 operation; no landfill; safer; meets permit 100% of time at a fraction of the cost).
- Must expand the project boundaries to fully account for all benefits such as ecosystem services (life cycle costing).
- Green infrastructure projects require different technical skills than the traditional gray alternative.
- Since green infrastructure solutions were not widely accepted when this was adopted, it required someone with passion to really drive and support the project. Upper management buy-in was a must.
- Need to have data to support a green infrastructure – this may point to needing more pilot-scale work in the general area of green infrastructure.
- The proper assessment of the 'full value' of the green infrastructure may help in the alternative assessment process and push green infrastructure project over gray ones.

Dow/TNC: air pollution mitigation via reforestation

Source/organisation: The Dow Chemical Company and The Nature Conservancy

Scale: Local, regional

Key stakeholder(s): Dow plant management, Environmental Protection Agency (EPA), Texas Commission on Environmental Quality (TCEQ), conservation community

Project phase: Research and evaluation stage

Geographical location: Houston-Galveston-Brazoria (HGB) area near Dow's Freeport Texas Operations

The Dow Chemical Company

PROJECT OVERVIEW

This project will produce a methodology for the use of reforestation for air quality maintenance or enhancement instead of, or in addition to, reducing emissions through end-of-pipe control technology or changes in operations. Forests could be part of the solution by modifying the environment and removing pollutants from the air.

Dow Texas Operations is located in the US Environmental Protection Agency (EPA)-designated Houston-Galveston-Brazoria (HGB) non-attainment area for ground-level ozone. The HGB region has been in violation of National Ambient Air Quality Standards (NAAQS) for ozone since the establishment of those standards in 1979. The HGB area failed to meet the revised 1997 NAAQS for ozone by the 2007 deadline, which has resulted in the mandatory imposition of Clean Air Act (CAA) penalty fees ($5,000/ton) on all large sources in the HGB area that exceed their allowed emission limits.

TECHNOLOGY MATURITY
Early: research and pilot stage.

Investment/costs/time
– 2-4 year pilot study.
– Reforestation and other costs TBD.

Project management considerations
– Identify suitable planting sites and tree species that also yield conservation benefits.
– Estimate removal of ozone and NO_2 by the reforestation project to estimate total NO_x credits the project could claim under the State Implementation Plan (SIP).
– Estimate the cost-effectiveness of the proposed green infrastructure solution (reforestation for NO_x control) to allow for comparison with alternative gray control methods. The analysis estimated NO_x abatement by a hypothetical planted forest, and found it was cost-competitive with the evaluated next round of 'gray' technology options that might be deployed should further NO_x controls be needed.
– Identify and estimate the value of additional benefits green infrastructure options offer.
– Need to get reforestation approved as an ozone precursor control strategy in ozone SIP (for the HGB area in this case).
– Work with appropriate federal and state regulators to increase likelihood of acceptance of and then ensure compliance with the proposed methodology.

Benefits
Anticipated:
– Reduced costs of additional ozone precursor abatement, if additional control efforts are deemed necessary to achieve compliance with National Ambient Air Quality Standards for ozone.
– Improved public services such as recreational opportunities for local residents and visitors and habitat for rare species.
– Air quality improvements which could lead to improved human and environmental health such as:
  • Carbon sequestration by the forest helps mitigates greenhouse gas emissions contributing to efforts to manage atmospheric concentrations of carbon and possibly creating value from pollution offsets or credits.
  • Reduced ground-level ozone formation (a smog-related pollutant) by mediating the urban heat island effect, leading to reduced energy use for space cooling, resulting in reduced pollutant emissions from power plants.

Risks/challenges
- Reforestation still needs to be approved by agencies as a strategy for air quality compliance. This requires that emission reductions be quantifiable, additional, enforceable and permanent. This requires verification of approaches, validation of the complex models involved and a thorough risk assessment analysis.
- Trees naturally emit volatile organic compounds (VOCs), which may lead to increased formation of ozone. This can be avoided if reforestation projects are sited in areas where ozone formation is NO_x-limited.
- Emissions from tree maintenance activities can also contribute to air pollution, so reforestation projects must be planned to minimise maintenance needs. This is achieved by designing such projects to be self-sustaining early on, using ecologically appropriate species, and planting forests rather than street or neighbourhood trees.
- If ex-post verification of estimated pollution removal reveals that actual removal is less than originally estimated, offset quantities would be reduced and the cost-effectiveness of reforestation as a control strategy would be less than originally estimated, and possibly may fall below that of conventional control approaches.

Resilience aspects
- Adding another option to the solution set increases flexibility while potentially reducing marginal costs.
- Stronger collaboration links with regulators increase social and governmental participation and thereby societal resilience.
- Forests damaged by extreme weather events or fire require more time to replace than gray solutions.
- Gray solutions are susceptible to events such as power loss and mechanical failure.

Key learning
- This proposal deals with a novel GI solution requiring testing and by in from a multitude of stakeholders and will therefore require a long period of study.
- Early stage – to be determined later in pilot, implementation, integration phases.
- Using reforestation for ozone abatement has broad relevance: a high share of the total area of ozone non-attainment and maintenance in the US is NO_x-limited and thus may be suitable for ozone removal through reforestation.

Shell: produced water treatment using reed beds

Source/organisation: Petroleum Development Oman LLC (PDO): joint venture with The Shell Petroleum Company Ltd and the Government of Oman (majority)

Scale: Large – world's largest commercial wetland covering more than 360 ha and treats more than 95,000 m³ of produced water per day

Key stakeholder(s): Government of Oman, BAUER Nimr LLC, Oman (a subsidiary of BAUER Resources GmbH in Germany).

Project phase: The plant came online in late 2010.

Geographical location: Nimr, Oman (Nimr is located inland in south-west Oman)

PROJECT OVERVIEW

At the PDO Nimr oil fields, a tenth of the total production is crude oil. The remaining production, around 330,000 m³ per day, is water that is brought to the surface together with the oil. This water used to be disposed of by injection into a deep disposal well. To reduce the high costs of treating and re-injecting the produced water, PDO together with BAUER, developed a project proposal that would reduce or eliminate the power consumption and CO_2 emissions associated with the operation of equipment for deep well disposal. The solution was a four-tier gravity-based wetland design.

As gravity pulls the water downhill, the reeds act as filters, removing oil from the water. The oil is eaten by microbes that naturally feed on hydrocarbons underground. Locally grown *Phragmites australis* plants are used for the purification of produced water. The composition of the produced water from the Nimr oilfield is brackish; with total dissolved solids (TDS) ranging between 7,000 mg/l and 8,000 mg/l, and the oil in water content varies between 100 to 500 mg/l. The plant layout includes a pipeline, which enters the NWTP system and leads to an oil/water separator. The water is then distributed into a wetland facility where it is channelled through four wetland terraces by gravity feed. Finally, evaporation ponds are used to recover the salt while the biomass is land filled. Alternative uses of the water and biomass that could offer a variety of environmental and socio-political benefits are being explored.

The constructed wetland is designed to treat 95,000 m³ per day (30% of the daily volume of water produced by the oilfield). The facility was constructed under a build-own-operate contract and as such, BAUER designed and built the facility and is now operating it for a 20-year period.

As with every effluent treatment plant, the subsoil must be properly sealed. In selecting suitable sealants, synthetic materials were rejected in favour of a natural product. The surrounding desert areas were searched for suitable clay until an appropriate sealant mixture was found.

A pilot study was used to evaluate and optimise reed bed efficiency. The reed beds have proven to be capable of efficiently, and cost-effectively, handling the treatment of the produced water from the Nimr oilfields.

TECHNOLOGY MATURITY
Proven; fully operational since late 2010.

INVESTMENT/COSTS/TIME
– The project required a pilot study of more than 2 years.
– The wetland was fully operational 2 years after the contract was awarded.

PROJECT MANAGEMENT CONSIDERATIONS
– Project selection criteria: capital and operational cost reductions, lowering the carbon footprint.
– Construction time of the wetland was roughly half of the traditional, gray infrastructure.
– Pilot studies involved recording and determining temperature, evaporation and evapo-transpiration rates as these can highly influence the performance of the constructed wetland.
– Pilot studies also investigated throughput parameters like retention time and hydraulic load for winter and summer seasons.

Benefits

– Significant capital cost savings compared to the man-made produced water treatment and injection facility.
– The gravity-based wetland design requires close to zero energy for water treatment, thus reducing power consumption by approximately 98% (for the 30 vol% of water treatment) due to the elimination of electric powered water treatment and injection equipment. Also, the new facility enables an additional crude oil recovery of 200 barrels per day.
– Satisfactory water treatment performance ever since the start of the wetland operation (December 2010). The oil content in the produced water is consistently reduced from 400 mg/l to less than 0.5 mg/l when leaving the wetland system.
– CO_2 emissions reduced by approximately 98% (for the 30 vol% of water treatment) due to the elimination of electric powered water treatment and injection equipment.
– The wetlands provide habitat for fish and hundreds of species of migratory birds. Also, the wetlands offer potential for innovative customer value propositions that could provide a variety of socio-political benefits e.g. through by-product optimisation (fresh water, biomass etc.).

Risks/challenges

– Large required land footprint: more than 360 ha to treat 95,000 m³/d of produced water.
– Long pilot period (>2 years) required to de-risk the constructed wetland technology and find the optimum wetland design.
– Operational risk of the wetland: potential risk of not meeting the performance requirements due to external factors (e.g. seasonal temperature swings, biotic stresses).

Resilience aspects

– This system is modular and the capacity can be increased stepwise.
– Potential for achieving improved system resilience by increasing biodiversity (using various types of reeds).
– The facility makes use of feedback loops for monitoring the health and efficacy of the wetland system.

Key learning

– Climate data and local soil conditions are essential design parameters.
– A champion was required to push this project even with positive results from the pilot study.

- It's important to involve other key stakeholders in the project (e.g. universities).
- It's recommended to use a non-biased project evaluation process to select the best available solution.

Shell: natural reclamation and erosion control for onshore pipelines

Source/organisation: Shell Canada Limited

Scale: Large – several reclamation plots are located in the Deep Basin Ojay Project site. The Ojay pipeline has eight reclamation research sites each approximately 20 metres wide by 100 metres long.

Key stakeholder(s): British Columbia government (Oil and Gas Commission), First Nation communities, ReClaimit Ltd (execution contractor)

Project phase: Fully implemented, has been operational for three years; optimisation studies ongoing

Geographical location: NE British Columbia, Canada

PROJECT OVERVIEW

Shell's projects often involve the construction of pipeline corridors in ecologically diverse areas on previously undeveloped lands called 'greenfield' development. The pipeline is routed along what is known as a 'right of way'.

When building a pipeline, the construction activities not only cover the civil works to lay the pipeline and build the pump/compressor stations, but also the reclamation work to return disturbed land to an equivalent land capability with minimal impact on the environment. There is heightened recognition and popularity of natural reclamation and soil erosion abatement techniques as these ancient techniques address the shortfalls related to man-made pipeline protection techniques, particularly in terms of reduced installation and maintenance costs.

The technique of using living plant materials to create structures that perform some soil related engineering function is referred to as soil 'bioengineering'. Often, soil bioengineering is used to treat sites where surface stability and erosion problems exist. Bioengineering solutions can be applied to a wide variety of sites disturbed by construction activities. These solutions use natural components of pioneering plant communities and thus align well with ecological restoration strategies.

It is preferred to use local plant species to construct soil bioengineering solutions for naturally disturbed sites. Some recent innovations in reclamation approaches include the use of willows and other tree/shrub/plant species to control soil erosion and establish a re-naturalisation path. In the past 15 years, Shell has proven success in willow staking in several upstream projects. Poplars and willows are highly valued for erosion control and efficient control of groundwater due to their rapid growth, high rooting capacity, extensive root systems and high water use.

Shell continues to investigate different reclamation methods, using direct seeding, nursery stock grown from native seed and possibly peat pucks (seed with nutrients), to better understand the feasibility of the technology as well as the costs and time involved in growing such solutions.

Pipeline projects involve many stakeholders with specific interests and concerns. The pipeline right of way often traverses lands with rights of use belonging to multiple indigenous communities. The indigenous communities are often concerned with the fragmentation of the land and its impacts on the local ecosystem. Therefore, all solutions are strictly reviewed with these local concerns in mind.

TECHNOLOGY MATURITY
Proven, with improvements being developed.

INVESTMENT/COSTS/TIME
– Natural reclamation techniques have the added benefit of having significantly lower costs than concrete and metal piling methods.
– Timelines for implementation generally fit very well with the overall project timeline as pipeline construction and tree planting share a common seasonal criteria and the activities can therefore be executed within the same timeframe.

PROJECT MANAGEMENT CONSIDERATIONS
– Natural reclamation does not provide a broad base solution, i.e. it is only applicable to certain sites.
– Project teams need to be willing to assess such alternative approaches.
– Natural reclamation solutions require different skill sets (horticulture, biology).

- Joining forces with external experts is critical for the success of these pilot studies.
- It is important to build relationships with all key stakeholders early on in the project.
- It is important to identify and mitigate local environmental risks (e.g. care was taken to maintain moose habitat in the harvested areas by leaving clumps of willows standing).
- Timing is key for success of this solution (e.g. when to cut and plant willows).
- It is important to secure manual labour for large scale projects.
- Reclamation is often a compliance-driven sustainability effort.

BENEFITS
- Lower overall environmental impact, potentially including CO_2 offsets.
- Solutions are known to be superior overtime compared to the more traditional stabilisation methods.
- Hands-on work can be structured as a team building/educational activity for Shell employees.
- Job creation for local labour.
- The solution can be designed to be sensitive to the local environment (e.g. allow access to local wildlife).
- These green solutions do not require regular maintenance as compared to gray solutions that often require mechanical intervention, e.g. for the excavation of existing banks or transport of materials.
- Low operating and maintenance cost.

RISKS/CHALLENGES
- Not a one-stop solution, but very much site specific (dependent on soil types, moisture level, light, etc.).
- Requires a different skill set for the design and implementation phase.
- Time constraints: any project would need to be started as early in the winter as possible.
- Survivability of the planting sites is an important requirement to establish long-term success.

RESILIENCE ASPECTS
- The green solution self-repairs and improves performance over time as opposed to gray solutions that depreciate over time and require maintenance.

- Solutions are modular; it is easy to select the required planting density along the pipeline corridor.
- Solutions are multi-functional: they reduce loss and fragmentation of wildlife habitat, reduce soil compaction and improve land capability and productivity in agricultural, prairie and forested areas.
- These types of natural re-vegetation systems reduce anthropogenic disturbances to local ecosystems.

KEY LEARNING
- The environmental agencies are very focused on achieving sustainable outcomes and are typically sympathetic to soft engineering solutions.

Shell/TNC: coastal pipeline erosion control using oyster reefs

Source/organisation: Shell Pipeline Company LP

Scale: Approximately one mile of shoreline in total, the pilot project will be designed with the intention to be replicated at other similar sites

Key partner(s): Shell Global Solutions International, The Nature Conservancy

Project phase: Feasibility study ongoing; final decision to proceed or not will be taken mid-2013, pending approval/acceptance of the design

Geographical location: Ship Shoal, Louisiana, USA

© *Seth Blitch for The Nature Conservancy*

PROJECT OVERVIEW

Attenuation of soil and marshland erosion around oil and gas pipelines located on or near shorelines is a chronic concern for Shell and other commercial operators in the Gulf of Mexico. Erosion is caused by waves from marine traffic, tidal currents, and acute weather events like hurricanes. Maintaining these pipelines currently requires an intensive and expensive monitoring and maintenance system. The traditional gray approach uses hardened structures that armour and stabilise the shoreline; rock reinforcement, wood and metal structures, sand or cement bags to slow erosion, particularly in high energy environments.

The main drawbacks of this existing system from the company's perspective are the costs and risks related to maintenance activities taking place around these hardened man-made structures. There is the ongoing risk of pipeline damages related to frequent boat traffic, as well as the loss of intertidal habitat.

To lower these costs and the overall risks to the pipeline, Shell and The Nature Conservancy have been exploring shoreline erosion control methods using natural infrastructure to further attenuate erosion from waves. The final project may encompass a hybrid solution using a combination of green and gray infrastructure.

Technology maturity

There is empirical evidence that supports that green infrastructure can be an effective measure against shoreline erosion and wave energy. The innovation lies in applying the concept of green infrastructure to more effectively protect pipelines from coastal erosion while offering multiple environmental and social benefits.

Investment/costs/time

A primary objective of this pilot project is to better understand the relative costs of using these methods and test the hypotheses that natural infrastructure is more cost-effective than made-made infrastructure. Historically, green infrastructure installations, such as oyster reef breakwaters, have cost approximately $1 million per mile versus $1.5 to $3 million per mile to install traditional gray rock barriers, though this is highly variable. GI solutions are expected to require lower initial capital costs and lower maintenance costs due to being inherently self-sustaining.

Project management considerations

The approach taken thus far has been to hold workshops and meetings to design this project as a joint effort between Shell Global Solutions International, Shell Pipeline Company LP and experts from The Nature Conservancy. The team organised a field visit and gathered location-specific data as part of the bid process to generate conceptual proposals for the Ship Shoal pipeline. Due to the importance of pipeline integrity, an internal risk analysis will be performed on the proposed solutions.

Selection criteria for the proposals are: installation/maintenance cost savings, efficiency in sediment accumulation for stabilisation, innovative edge and the delivery of ecosystem services.

Benefits

- Creates a natural buffer to protect the shoreline and pipeline from erosion.
- Can preserve and/or create habitat for benthic, estuarine, shallow water, and intertidal organisms.
- Increases stability for pipelines.
- Improves local water quality.
- Lowers installation and maintenance costs compared to gray solutions.
- Offers potential for local job creation.

- Creates land behind the natural defences (open water to marsh; marsh to land).
- Has potential for self-repairing (fixes cracks developed from potential storm) and self-organising structure (oyster bed builds up with sea level rise).

RISKS/CHALLENGES

- It is important to understand the business case (green vs gray).
- Shell's comfort level with long-term liability issues (public access to a newly created oyster bed is a concern).
- GI solutions will need to comply with company and industry standards and requirements.
- These novel approaches require receptiveness of both internal and external stakeholders.
- There may be a need to train new contractors who may not be familiar with designing and installing natural infrastructure.
- The greatest concern may be related to social stresses such as pressure from oyster fishermen who could harvest and potentially inhibit natural growth and effectiveness.

RESILIENCE ASPECTS

- GI solutions have the dynamic capacity to repair themselves and adapt to evolving chronic and acute stressors. For example, in response to rising water levels due to climate change, an oyster reef will grow to match the new water levels, unlike any gray infrastructure.
- GI solutions offer multi-functional benefits, such as oyster beds providing erosion control and other ecosystem services.

KEY LEARNING

- The keys to success for these kinds of methods will be finding the appropriate project scale, managing any regulatory constraints, proving long-term benefits, proving effectiveness at sediment accumulation and wave attenuation thereby protecting the pipeline, and creating a replicable product and process.
- A successful pilot should resolve most of the institutional, regulatory and financial concerns.
- Key anticipated lessons relate to testing the hypotheses that green infrastructure can be a superior alternative to gray infrastructure in protecting pipelines in the Gulf of Mexico, and better understanding under what circumstances green infrastructure and/or a hybrid combination of green/gray infrastructure is a cost-effective investment.

TNC: Cauca Valley water fund[1]

Green infrastructure type: Water treatment using forest and land management

Source/organisation: The Nature Conservancy

Scale: Seven small watersheds

Key stakeholder(s): The water fund is overseen by the Cauca Valley's sugar cane producers association (ASOCANA), the sugar cane growers association (PROCANA), each watershed's local environmental authority, Vallenpaz (a peace and justice organisation) and The Nature Conservancy.

Project phase: Established in 2009, projects and investments are underway

Geographical location: Regional around Cali, Colombia; mostly Valle del Cauca Department

© *Timothy Boucher/TNC for The Nature Conservancy*

PROJECT OVERVIEW

The East Cauca Valley Water Fund is one of the more recently established water funds in Latin America. Water Funds are a financial vehicle developed at TNC, where main water users put resources into the fund and then the fund chooses projects to invest directly in the watershed.

The funds focus on investing in three types of services: water quality, sediment retention and water quantity. Typical investments include: changing land use or intensity (such as less intensive agriculture and ranching); fencing, creating silvopastoral systems, forest enrichment and restoration,

1   Calvache (2009), Goldman (2010), Padilla (2011), Ramos, Benitez and Calvache (2012), Tallis and Calvache (2011)

enhancing protected areas; land acquisitions; and restoring riparian areas, slopes, and corridors for biodiversity (Ramos, Benitez and Calvache 2012).

A recent ecosystem services analysis of the Bogota Water Fund determined that ranching and agricultural lands produce 10% more sediments than areas under conservation. That sediment increase requires approximately $4 to $5 million in additional water treatment costs downstream for end users.

The East Cauca Valley Water Fund was established around the private sector as sugar cane producers and growers in the region entered into a voluntary payment scheme to finance green projects across seven watersheds. Based in the Valle region of Colombia, the fund establishes a payment for ecosystem services for the growers based on hectares and tons of sugar cane produced. The cane growers were motivated to invest by research predicting that, without direct intervention, within ten years they would be forced to reduce their irrigation cycles from five to four, potentially losing US$33 million per year. So far, the primary investments by the fund have been in changing land use or intensity; fencing, silvopastoral systems, forest enrichment and restoration.

The gray alternatives to the kinds of projects supported by these water funds include: building more dams (water quantity), treatment plants (water quality) or new pipelines for water supply from other watersheds.

TECHNOLOGY MATURITY

Science papers show that investments in watersheds improve water quality and sediment retention and improve or maintain base flows. Furthermore, the financial mechanism has proven to be efficient with the Quito Water Fund, Fondo para la Protection del Agua (FONAG, 11 years old, endowment of nearly $10 million). The Conservancy alone has created 11 funds with approximately 30 more in the pipeline; analysis of green versus gray is pending.

INVESTMENT/COSTS/TIME

The East Cauca Valley Water Fund has committed to investing $10 million over the next 5 years (Tallis and Calvache 2011). For the mature Quito Water Fund (FONAG) approximately 2% of the water utility revenue is paid into the fund. Some of the utility fees go to the endowment while the rest goes directly to project implementation.

Establishing an endowment is important to make long-term agreements on watershed, with farmers, etc. The Quito-FONAG Fund is currently investing $2 million and can leverage $2 million to $4 million (FONAG 2010).

The disadvantage for green infrastructure is in the startup and initial financing capacity: the East Cauca Valley Water Fund currently has annual revenues of $1 million to $2 million but the business plan states that $18 million is needed for many projects to achieve very significant regional outcomes, which will take 12 to 15 years to raise. The timeline for outcomes is also problematic as some of these projects will take 20 to 30 years to mature while stakeholders expect results within ten years.

PROJECT MANAGEMENT CONSIDERATIONS
The process developed by the water fund and The Conservancy for determining how investments should be made is as follows: (1) choose objectives: through negotiation; (2) choose activities: based on science and experience; (3) allocate budget: based on experience; (4) conduct a diagnostic screen: ranking of projects; (5) select priority areas: return on investment; (6) estimate returns: using models; (7) design monitoring programme; (8) implement project. The fund uses the GIS-based InVEST model suite developed as part of the Natural Capital Project to identify priority areas for intervention. (Tallis and Calvache 2011; Ramos, Benitez and Calvache 2012).

The entire process is managed by a board of directors (ideally, 50% public and 50% private governance) and guided by annual and long-term plans. Water funds identify watershed areas and projects that give the highest ROI for water quality, sediment retention, and/or water quantity. TNC and several funds are also exploring water pollution as an additional key metric to target in the future.

BENEFITS
– Increased water supply.
– Flood risk management.
– Increased agricultural productivity.
– Reduced waste and nutrient production and improved treatment.
– Social benefits: environmental education, local entrepreneurship, commercialisation of facilities.
– The Water Fund approach is much faster in terms of planning and impact versus gray options:
  • Gray is government-driven and can take upwards of 10+ years to commence projects.
  • Green can also be integrated into gray infrastructure and planning.
– Insurance costs (possible positive impact, needs research).
– Risk management changes/improvements for the private sector.

- In Medellín, Colombia, several large industrial companies are exploring Water Fund-style projects to reduce their operational and reputational risk from dangerous bacteria blooms in their water supply.

RISKS/CHALLENGES
- Governance issues; questions over who manages the fund, efficiency concerns:
  - Necessary to build alliances with utilities and key users.
- Need local government stability and buy-in.
- Need sound conservation agreements with the local communities; rule of law.
- Need to capitalise/begin projects quickly (two to three years) but results can take time to materialise.

RESILIENCE ASPECTS
- The field needs more research and modelling to compare green versus gray techniques in terms of resilience before any definitive judgements can be made. However, initial results and most experts believe the green techniques will be more energy efficient and require less maintenance than the traditional gray approaches.
- Resilience and flexibility in response to the effects of climate change could further tip the scales in favour of more green approaches and Water Fund-type projects.
- A Water Fund offers a more bottom-up approach in contrast to gray infrastructure (government planned) which empowers end users to invest in future, e.g. sugar cane growers.

KEY LEARNING
- Green disadvantage is in the startup and initial financing capacity:
  - Water for Life currently has annual revenues of $1 million to $2 million but business plan says $18 million is needed for many projects with the most significant outcomes, which will take 12 to 15 years to raise. Need to show results in 10 years instead of 20 to 30.
- It is essential to identify the beneficiaries and water users, but not necessary to engage all stakeholders early on (start with the big users first to build momentum).
- Getting the basic science in place is essential and more work must be done to quantify the benefits whenever possible, communicate them to stakeholders, and frame the benefits, goals, costs, etc. into a science-based business plan.

TNC: integrated reservoir-floodplain management

Source/organisation: The Nature Conservancy

Scale: Regional; application over the whole of a river basin

Key stakeholder(s): Army Corps of Engineers, Institute for Water Resources, Hydrologic Engineering Center, TNC, University of California-Davis

Project phase: Study complete, implementation being explored on the Mokelumne River (California) and Cedar River (Iowa). Full implementation phase requires governance/financial mechanisms/political leadership to occur.

Geographical location: Examples: Savannah River (Georgia/South Carolina); Mokelumne River (California)

© *Jerry and Marcy Monkman for The Nature Conservancy*

Project overview

Most of the tens of thousands of large dams around the world are not designed for a single purpose, but instead must balance flood protection, water supply, hydroelectric power generation, and other demands. These demands on water management often compete. One of the most common trade-offs involves choosing between keeping reservoirs relatively empty to reduce downstream flood risk or keeping them relatively full to provide water for cities and farms, generate hydropower, and support recreation. This conflict can be reduced and overall social benefits increased by restoring the natural flood storage and conveyance that downstream floodplains provide, thereby enabling the reallocation of some reservoir flood storage to other purposes.

This project investigates the possible benefits of coupling reservoir operations with floodplain management. The study components include modelling scenarios of incremental reductions in reservoir flood storage (0-100%), calculating incremental flood damages associated with flood-storage changes and quantifying the cost to mitigate those damages via floodplain management, assessing the benefits associated with reallocating flood storage to other purposes (water supply, hydropower generation, recreation and environment), and developing business propositions including financial models highlighting the costs and benefits of reallocating reservoir flood storage in coordination with changes in downstream floodplain management. This study was performed on two very different case study rivers – the Savannah basin and the Mokelumne basin.

- Research the integration of the green and gray infrastructure for flood risk management and floodplain service provision.
- Proposed interventions: change allocation of reservoir storage; adjust dam operations; change flood plain management, land uses, relocation, etc.; move and/or enhancing levees.
- Proposed reducing dam flood water storage by 25%, 50%, 75% and 100%.
- Taking some of the reservoir storage away from flood control (via floodplains) allows you to keep more of the reservoir water storage for water supply, recreation and other uses.
- Reallocating water storage away from flood control results in substantial social benefits in both basins, including a 25-50% reallocation in the Mokelumne that would provide water supply for an additional 450,000 people (a major issue in California). The same 25-50% reallocation in the Savannah River would allow for increased hydroelectric generation valued at more than $12 million per year and enhanced recreation worth $3 million per year.

TECHNOLOGY MATURITY
Research and pilot phases; a decade-long collaboration on dam operations and supporting work on floodplain management and policy.

INVESTMENT/COSTS/TIME
- Significant: floodplain land use changes, land acquisitions or easements; policy changes for broad implementation; potentially Congressional lobbying.
- Savannah (Georgia and South Carolina, USA): Small changes in floodplain management enable the use of up to 50% of the existing flood storage to increase hydropower and recreation valued at nearly US$13 million per year with no increased flood risk and with additional benefits for water supply, recreation, the environment, and climate change resilience.

– Mokelumne (California, USA): Modest shifts in floodplain management free 25% to 50% of upstream reservoir flood storage for public water supply – enough additional water for nearly 450,000 people – while maintaining flood protection, increasing hydropower generation, and improving habitat for declining salmon.

PROJECT MANAGEMENT CONSIDERATIONS
– The knowledge and tools exist to support full implementation of this approach in river basins around the world.
– Analysis can be furthered by including considerations of dam mainte-nance, safety and ecosystem services recognised but still not valued, as well as more rigorous assessment of costs-benefits under climate change futures.
– Must overcome the hurdles of governance systems/financial mechanisms and political leadership.
– The policy changes to enable fuller implementation are not complicated, but the politics are a challenge around private land use issues. However, these are potentially overcome through use of incentive-based finance mechanisms rather than government 'takings'. More feasible in areas where floodplain is mostly undeveloped lands or agriculture with fewer stakeholders.

BENEFITS
– Reduced flood risk and flood damages through mitigation of properties currently most at risk.
– Increased water supply (quality and quantity); current reservoir flood storage in the United States is a large enough volume to meet the annual water needs of 800+ million Americans, so reallocating even 10-20% of that volume is game-changing.
– Additional hydropower revenue.
– Increase revenue from additional recreational use.

RISKS/CHALLENGES
– High-levels of engagement with Army Corps of Engineers and potentially from Congress to authorise significant changes in reservoir plans, dam operations, and authority/funding for land acquisitions/easements, etc.
– Army Corps does not have authority over floodplain land uses.
– Social needs conflict on the landscape. Example: After a dam is con-structed, communities develop along river banks in higher flood risk areas.

– Approach currently is not practical in areas with a high level of human development due to large investment required and complexity involved in relocating houses/businesses/farms.
– Requires strong political will from local leaders and community.
– Perverse incentives for certain kinds of agricultural production that impact floodplains (Farm Bill: crop insurance); these incentives could be shifted to be positive.
– Economic losses for land use changes (e.g. removal of farmland from use) and flood risk changes.
– National Flood Insurance Program (NFIP) needs to incorporate a risk-based approach; initial changes along these lines were made by Congress in NFIP this summer.
– Flooding continues to occur despite the continued large investment in gray infrastructure, warranting a change of approach (likely catalyst for change).

RESILIENCE ASPECTS
– Multi-functional: by reallocating reservoir storage, increase resilience to water supply/energy from hydropower/flood control onto the floodplains. Enhances social and ecosystem health.
– Various downstream benefits from ecosystem services not yet valued.
– Unlike floodplains, current gray infrastructure is rigid and vulnerable to breaching during acute events or recurrent droughts, often with a breaking point (e.g. Army Corps designed Mississippi levees).
– Modular: restoration of floodplains can be built in modular form, e.g. floodplains can serve as a sustainable and controlled relief valve by opening up certain critical areas of levees. Preferential flooding (relief value) can benefit highly populated urban areas. This is exactly what the corps did – by design – on the Mississippi in 2011.
– Improved operational flexibility to meet environmental flow targets and to adapt to more frequent and intense floods and droughts.
– Great example of hybrid solution: grey infrastructure (dam) already in place can be coupled with green infrastructure (floodplain restoration) to reach higher level of resilience.

KEY LEARNING
Changing dam operations in coordination with floodplain management can increase social, economic and environmental benefits, including improved water supply and water quality, increased hydropower, enhanced flood protection, restored environmental health, expanded recreational opportunities, and increased resilience to the impacts of climate change.

TNC: managing storm water runoff with wetlands[2]

Source/organisation: The Nature Conservancy

Scale: Municipalities

Key stakeholder(s): Water Department, TNC, NRDC, EKO Asset Management Partners

Project phase: Early implementation, extensive planning

Geographical location: Philadelphia, Pennsylvania, USA

© Tim Pierce at commons.Wikimedia.org

PROJECT OVERVIEW

Philadelphia has a sewer collection system that is 60% combined sewer and 40% municipal separate storm sewer system. The city is working to improve storm water management and alleviate pressure on this combined sewer system (CSS) through restoration and demonstration efforts, regulations and incentives for the private sector via a revised storm water billing system. Philadelphia is trying to institutionalise green infrastructure as standard practice via citywide policies, such as a parcel-based billing system for commercial properties, Green Plan Philadelphia, Green Roof Tax Credit and the Green Streets programme (EPA 2010).

- Philadelphia is one of 200 cities that are not in EPA compliance on storm water overflow, whereby raw sewage goes into combined sewer systems and then into waterways.
- EPA fines are a strong regulatory and financial driver in the US for cities to take action.
- Philadelphia forecasts expenditures of $10 billion to solve their storm water problem over the next decade using gray infrastructure; the same estimate using green infrastructure is $2 billion (Natural Resources Defense Council et al. 2013)

- • City leaders are committed to green infrastructure solving a significant portion (20-30%) of this problem for less than costs of traditional gray infrastructure.
- – Examples of green infrastructure include rain barrels, bioswales, pervious pavement, wetland protection and restoration; and other means to increase infiltration or retain rain water to reduce peak flow.
- – Philadelphia set a new water billing system for commercial and industrial properties based on the amount of impervious surface on properties; also owners can get a fee credit through implementation of storm water.
- – PWD has allocated $1.67 billion, on an inflation-adjusted basis, over a 25-year period to green at least 9,564 acres across the city, pursuant to a consent order with the Pennsylvania Department of Environmental Protection (Natural Resources Defense Council et al. 2013).

Technology
Maturity: mature.

Investment/costs/time
- – Revised storm water billing system based the amount of a commercial property's impervious cover and thereby the amount of runoff a property will generate.
- – City offers a storm water fee discount for customers who reduce impervious cover using green infrastructure practices.
- – There are multiple ways to finance green storm water management including public-private partnerships, offsite credit trading, etc. (Natural Resources Defense Council et al. 2013).

Project management considerations
- – Metrics used: cost savings.
- – Local political leadership is key.
- – See *Creating Clean Water Cash Flows: Developing Private Markets for Green Stormwater Infrastructure in Philadelphia* for a detailed analysis and recommendations for investment in green infrastructure for stormwater management (Natural Resources Defense Council et al. 2013).

Benefits
- – Storm water runoff reduction resulting in water quality improvements, relief to aging gray infrastructure.
- – Create habitat for wildlife; carbon sequestration; recreation dual use spaces (ex. baseball fields).

– New practices will reduce combined sewer overflow (CSO) by 25 billion gallons, and save the city as much as $8 billion over gray infrastructure alternatives.

RISKS/CHALLENGES
– Evaluation of green solutions takes longer, can be more expensive and complex; gray is a known, easier.
– Comfort level of regulators with these newer projects (Philadelphia fought for years for a consent decree). Regulators can be concerned over precedent and 'slippery slope' problems.
– Financing challenge for both green and gray; green is generally cheaper.
– Green projects are more visible and potentially polarising whereas the gray option is invisible; alternatively, the green options can create community assets that benefit people.

RESILIENCE ASPECTS
– In general resilience of either approach is similar but adding green to existing gray CSS can provide buffer and add filtration benefits.
– Gray advantage: harder to add capacity to a wetland than it is to increase pipe size.
– Energy uses are comparable after construction; gray requires much energy more to build.
– Green produces less waste as wetlands can also filter and absorb waste.
– Maintenance is much less for green.
– Green filters most pollutants on site.
– Acute stress: A flood can overwhelm both. Green might be more flood-tolerant and will not lose all function like a burst pipe.

KEY LEARNING
– Mayors have a large role to play in bringing GI to the table for municipalities.
– Financial incentives could be optimised by taxing impervious surfaces differently based on geography.
– Green co-benefits can be time consuming to evaluate and value.
– Green can complement gray infrastructure, buffer the worst storm surges.
– Green infrastructure represents cost advantage versus building new CSS capacity.
– Different skill set is required to fully understand/need to educate the key stakeholders.

TNC: oyster reef building and restoration for coastal protection[3]

Source/organisation: The Nature Conservancy

Scale: Local. Miles of oyster reefs installed in the Gulf of Mexico

Key stakeholder(s): Natural Capital Project, donor organisations, local communities, enterprises

Project phase: Several successful project sites, expanding in use as experience and technology evolve

Geographical location: Gulf of Mexico, potentially other sites as well. Oysters are found around the world in temperate and tropical waters. They develop some of the greatest structures in places like the Gulf of Mexico, the Atlantic seaboard up to New York, as well as waters off China, Japan and in similar Southern Hemisphere oceans.

© *Daniel White for The Nature Conservancy*

PROJECT OVERVIEW

Oyster reefs have lost an estimated 85% of their historic extent globally (Beck et al. 2011). This loss carries a high economic cost because of the wide range of benefits oyster reefs provide to humans. Growing research on reef restoration in the last decade suggests that such restoration is feasible on a large scale, holding the prospect of recovery of ecosystem services and economic benefits. For a large reef restoration project in Mobile Bay, Alabama, for example, TNC conservatively estimated that 5,850 m of restored reefs:

– Produce over 3,100 kg of finfish and crab and 3,460 kg of oyster (meat) harvests per year.

3   Beck (2011), Kroeger (2012), Kroeger and Guannel (2014)

- Reduce the height and energy at shoreline of the average and top 10% of waves by 53-91% and 76-99%, respectively.
- Remove up to 1,888 kg of nitrogen per year from surrounding nearshore waters.

Total net benefits (consumer and producer surplus) from fishery enhancement dominate overall benefits from the reefs along the currently undeveloped shores with an estimated $217,000-$225,000 per year and their net present value (NPV) exceeds restoration costs ($4.28 million) in year 34.

For 50- and 100-year lifetimes and counting only fishery benefits, the reefs have a combined social return on investment (ROI) of 1.3 and 1.8 and a NPV of $1.17 million and $3.23 million, respectively.

Given ambitious restoration plans, the ROI of reef restoration is expected to increase substantially due to knowledge gains and economies of scale. Especially along developed shorelines, the ROI of reef restoration may exceed that of single-purpose alternatives for coastal protection and fishery enhancement due to the multi-functionality of reefs (Kroeger 2012).

The Gulf of Mexico is the single best opportunity for large-scale restoration of oyster reefs and sustainable fisheries, even as there has been an 85% loss of oyster reef ecosystems around the world. Restoring oyster reefs can have positive benefits for storm surge protection and sea level rise, social and economic vulnerability and risk, and conservation.

- Proven value of wave attenuation, reducing the energy and height of waves; and just like any breakwater the function varies in space and time.
- Gulf of Mexico: 6+ miles of oyster reefs implemented as breakwater projects.
- Re(building) reefs is done on a base using bagged oyster shells (best option) and/or cement structures; this structure is then seeded with oysters.
- Storm surge protection benefits are immediate as this base, which is a hybrid or green and gray.
- Reefs are self-maintaining and can grow with sea-level change.

TECHNOLOGY MATURITY
Proven, for wave attenuation/storm protection. Now looking to optimise co-benefits like habitat, conservation, biodiversity, etc. But these benefits may take more time to prove.

INVESTMENT/COSTS/TIME
- Timeline varies slightly by geography because growth rates vary by species/strain of oyster, water conditions, etc.

- In Gulf of Mexico, benefits appear immediately after first stages of project (sinking bagged shells or concrete).
- Cost: About $1.5 million per mile, which is comparable or cheaper than gray alternatives in initial costs, with much higher cost/benefit returns because of the associated co-benefits
  - Gray infrastructure is industry- and profit-supported. Even Army Corps of Engineers has a bias toward gray. Engineers understand gray choices.
  - Reef restorations are often conducted by non-profit organisations, volunteer efforts and smaller startup companies, which may be one reason costs are as significantly lower.

PROJECT MANAGEMENT CONSIDERATIONS
- Project and identification materials and guidance: http://www.coastal-resilience.org/gulfmex
- Depth of water, salinity (oysters somewhat tolerant of variations), historical and current oyster populations.

BENEFITS
- Protection from waves and erosion is very clear; stabilisation of shorelines and even expansion of coasts. Storm surge protection and greater safety for people and property are highly likely given the engineering results from comparable structures (e.g. submerged breakwaters), but are not yet proven from direct evidence before and after storms (we simply have not had them in place for these events). The potential for lower insurance costs is also real.
- Additional fisheries production; more habitat produces more species and populations, including fish, crabs, shell fish.
- Shellfish filtration improves water quality.
- Changes in shoreline, such as increase in marsh abundance.
- Job creation for local workers, building/maintaining reefs.

RISKS/CHALLENGES
- People value oysters as a food source and harvesting slows progress.
- Growing oysters can smother sea grass habitat; possible conflict with other native habitat (in the Pacific Northwest). This is not an issue in the Gulf of Mexico.
- Shellfish industry is afraid of illegal harvesting in sub-optimal waters where oysters could be contaminated (these fears are exaggerated).

RESILIENCE ASPECTS
- Maintenance advantages (under study); still need to measure the repair/growth timeline and reduction in costs
  - Self-repair will be huge over time for both acute and chronic stresses.
  - Acute damage creates greater water flow around structure, which causes faster oysters growth.
- Oyster reefs will naturally expand upward with sea level, likely adjusting to chronic stresses (climate change).
- Lower energy requirements.
- Very popular with community, which sees value in protection, improved fish habitat.

KEY LEARNING
- No structure offers absolute protection, and there is a need to increase understanding of reefs and not overpromise on protection benefits.
- The case for oyster reef bed building and restoration is compelling. The Gulf of Mexico is the single best and maybe last place where oyster reef and fisheries can see value from new structures. Can build them big enough to be significant.
- Many reef projects are getting stimulus funding. Restoration creates jobs, so projects funded.
- Most projects had been reefs in front of natural areas. When these started showing results, then more green projects for replacing submerged breakwaters ensued with greater interest from municipalities. Now most reef projects are situated in front of developed areas.

Author biographies

Marco Albani is a Senior Expert in the Sustainability and Resource Productivity Practice of McKinsey & Company, where he serves clients in the public and private sectors on natural resources and sustainability topics, focussing on the land use sector and on the opportunities and challenges that climate change and resource constraints present for economic development and business strategies. Prior to joining McKinsey, Marco worked at Harvard University as a research scientist modelling carbon sequestration in forest ecosystems. Marco holds a PhD in Forest Sciences from the University of British Columbia and an MSc in Forest Sciences from the University of Florence.

Simone Arizzi is responsible for technology and innovation in the EMEA region. In this role he leads the definition and implementation of large technology-driven growth projects related to food, energy and protection; develops and executes the regional open innovation strategy with industrial partners and academic institutions; and drives the new initiative of the DuPont Innovation Centers. He joined DuPont in 1991 in Geneva and has held a variety of technology and business management positions, including global technology management in DuPont Photovoltaic Solutions from 2007-2012. He holds a chemical engineering degree from the ETH in Zürich and a PhD in chemical engineering from MIT.

Jaap Berghuijs currently works in the Reinsurance Strategy team at Swiss Re in Zurich. He joined the Resilience Action Initiative on behalf of Swiss Re's Sustainability unit in 2013 and previously interned as a Production Geologist at Royal Dutch Shell in the Netherlands. Jaap holds a BSc (cum laude) in Earth Sciences from Utrecht University and an MSc in Geology from the Swiss Federal Institute of Technology, ETH Zurich, where his thesis in physical volcanology was published and recognised with an award.

Maike Böggemann has been leading Shell's work on water-energy linkages since 2010. As part of the scenario team, she is deeply involved in Shell's internal policy, technology and capability discussions, as well as in external collaborations on the water-energy-food nexus with governments, the private sector, civil society and academics. Through this work she developed an interest in complex systems and resilience and a belief that collaboration and an improved understanding of interdependencies can create value for both society and business. At Shell since 1999, Maike's previous roles were in operations and supply-chain management in various Shell businesses. She holds a MSc in Logistics and Strategy from Erasmus University in Rotterdam. Maike co-authored a paper on water accounting for energy pathways in 2011/12.

Norbert Both has over fifteen years of experience in external communications and foreign policy. In 2006, Norbert left the Netherlands diplomatic service to join Shell, where he has served in various communications roles including Vice-President Corporate Communications. He has worked closely with successive CEOs on their external reputation agendas and with the Shell Business Environment team on driving a forward-looking agenda. Norbert obtained a PhD in International Relations from the University of Sheffield and co-authored the acclaimed book "Srebrenica: Record of a War Crime" (Penguin: 1996). From 2006-2014, he served as a member of the Board of the Netherlands Atlantic Association.

Since 2008, **David Bresch** heads the Sustainability unit at Swiss Re. He has been member of the deal teams for many innovative risk transfer transactions, like cat bonds and weather index solutions. David has been a member of the Swiss delegation to the UNFCCC climate negotiations from 2009 to 2012. He serves as member of the Private Sector Advisory Group of the UN Green Climate Fund. At the Swiss Federal Institute of Technology (ETH), he is a member of the industry advisory board of the Department of Environmental Sciences and is a lecturer on the economics of climate adaptation. David Bresch holds a PhD in physics from the ETH.

Maximilian Egger is Senior Consultant with Siemens AG, Munich, since 2012. Prior to this he was Country Manager and CEO of Siemens in Ukraine. Egger joined Siemens in 1972 as a project engineer and has held management positions in Siemens sales and service organisations in Germany, Libya, Singapore, Indonesia, Australia, Egypt, Romania and Ukraine ever since. He was born in Austria in 1953. He has Austrian and Australian citizenship. In 1972 he graduated from the Salzburg Technical College with a degree in electrical engineering. He holds a Doctor Honoris Causa degree from Donetsk National Technical University of Ukraine.

Rainer Egloff is a Senior Risk Manager in Swiss Re's Emerging Risk Management unit which is dedicated to early risk detection. He also serves as expert liaison to coordinate Swiss Re's input to the World Economic Forum's

Global Risks Report. Before joining Swiss Re in 2012, Rainer Egloff worked as a researcher at Collegium Helveticum, a scholarly institution devoted to transdisciplinarity, sponsored by ETH Zurich and University of Zurich. Rainer holds a Doctorate degree in history from the University of Zurich.

As Corporate Vice President, Sustainability, **Dr Neil Hawkins** drives strategy and implementation for sustainability and EH&S at Dow, including the enterprise-wide 2015 Sustainability Goals. Since 1988, he has served at Dow in a range of functional, business and operations roles. Hawkins is a widely-recognised authority on sustainable business, environmental policy and win-win solutions for business and ecosystems. He is a board member of numerous organisations; chairs the Strategic Advisory Council of the University of Michigan's Erb Institute for Global Sustainable Enterprise; and is a trustee of the Michigan chapter of The Nature Conservancy. Hawkins holds doctoral and master's degrees from Harvard University, and is an alumnus of Georgia Tech.

Kimberly Henderson is a consultant at McKinsey & Company focused on energy and climate change. She is currently based in London, coordinating the innovation research of the Global Commission on the Economy and Climate. Previously, she spent three years in São Paulo, Brazil, and worked with McKinsey clients across four continents. She loves languages, and is continually working to improve her Portuguese, Spanish and French. Kimberly has a BSc in Economics and Politics and an MSc in Environment and Development, both from the London School of Economics.

Roland Kupers, a theoretical physicist by training, is an independent consultant on complexity, resilience and energy transition, as well as an Associate Fellow at the Smith School of Enterprise and the Environment at the University of Oxford. He has spent a decade each in executive roles at AT&T and then at Royal Dutch Shell. He has published widely, including in HBR, on Project Syndicate and co-authored *The Essence of Scenarios* (with A. Wilkinson; Amsterdam, 2014) and *Complexity and the Art of Public Policy* (with D. Colander; Princeton, 2014). Roland was a co-author of a report commissioned by the German Government on a "New Growth Path for Europe".

Michel M. Liès is Swiss Re's Group CEO. Michel has built up a wealth of experience in the areas of life and non-life re/insurance since joining Swiss Re in 1978. He became a member of the Group's Executive Committee from 2005. As the Chairman Global Partnerships he focused on building and deepening long-term relationships with public sector stakeholders, governments and NGOs, with a particular focus on emerging markets. A citizen of Luxembourg, he is fluent in six languages. Michel holds a degree in mathematics from the Federal Institute of Technology in Zurich.

Herman van der Meyden is commercial advisor for Royal Dutch Shell in the Netherlands. His previous role was engineer at Shell's Prelude Floating LNG project. Before that, he contributed to the Shell Strategic Energy Scenarios, Scramble and Blueprints. Outside his job, Herman is co-founder of the Perspectivity Network, which explores new models of collaboration for an increasingly complex world. He is a board member at the oil and gas division of the Royal Dutch Institute of Engineers KIVI. He holds an MSc in Offshore Engineering from the Delft University of Technology and an MA in International Relations and Diplomacy from Leiden University.

Glenn Prickett is Chief External Affairs Officer at The Nature Conservancy (TNC), where he oversees international and US government relations, corporate engagements and relationships with leading international institutions and non-governmental organisations. Glenn joined TNC in 2010 after two decades working on environment and development policy at Conservation International and the Natural Resources Defense Council. As a senior fellow at the United Nations Foundation, Glenn helped develop an effective global response to climate change. He also has served as chief environmental advisor at the US Agency for International Development. Glenn holds a BA in economics and political science from Yale University.

Dawn Rittenhouse is Director Sustainability for the DuPont Company. Dawn joined DuPont in 1980 and has held positions in Technical Service, Sales, Marketing, and Product Management. In late 1997, she began to assist DuPont businesses in integrating sustainability into their strategy and business management processes. She leads DuPont's efforts at the WBCSD and the UNGC. She is currently on the Sustainability Council at Penn State's Smeal College of Business, GE's Sustainability Advisory Council, and the Board of Trustees of the Nature Conservancy of Delaware. Dawn has a double major in Chemistry and Economics from Duke University.

Mark Smith is the Director of the IUCN Global Water Programme. He leads IUCN's work on policy and practice related to water, environment and development. Prior to joining IUCN, Smith was a scientist with areas of specialisation in agriculture, forestry and hydrology. His research focused on agroforestry, first in West Africa and then in Kenya, while at Edinburgh University and the UK Centre for Ecology and Hydrology. He was leader of the interdisciplinary 'Livelihoods and Environment' research group at CSIRO Sustainable Ecosystems in Australia, supporting sustainable development in tropical river catchments, before becoming policy advisor on climate change and poverty at the UK development NGO Practical Action. Smith holds an undergraduate degree in Agriculture, an MA in Climatology and a PhD in Ecology.

Thekla Teunis works as a business developer at the Ecosystem Return Foundation in South Africa and as Director Africa for the Land Life Company. Previously she worked as a Strategy Consultant at McKinsey, and as a Stress Nexus Analyst in Shell's Group Strategy. Her activities focused on building on bottom-up initiatives to address the water-energy challenge through collaborative business models under the Resilience Action Initiative. In addition to her day job, she is co-founder and member of the board at Move and a member of the Global Shapers Community of the World Economic Forum. Thekla holds a BA in language and culture studies and a MSc in Mathematical Sciences from Utrecht University, both cum laude.

Peter Voser was CEO of Royal Dutch Shell from 2009 to 2013. He joined Shell in 1982 after graduating in business administration from the University of Applied Sciences, Zürich. He went on to work in a number of finance and business roles in Switzerland, UK, Argentina and Chile. Back in London from 1997, Peter held executive roles in the Oil Products division. He was CFO of ABB from 2002 until 2004, when he returned to Shell as CFO. Peter serves on the Board of Roche and is the Chairman of both the St Gallen Foundation and Catalyst. He also served on the Boards of Aegon and UBS and has been a member of the Swiss Federal Auditor Oversight Authority.

Brian Walker is an Honorary Fellow in Australia's CSIRO Ecosystems Sciences Division. He Chairs the Board of The Resilience Alliance (www.resalliance.org), has an appointment in the Stockholm Resilience Centre and is a Fellow of the Beijer Institute of Ecological Economics in Sweden. He lectured at the University of Zimbabwe, was Professor of ecology at the University of the Witwatersrand, South Africa, and Chief of CSIRO Wildlife and Ecology. He led the International Decade of the Tropics Program on savannas for six years and the Global Change and Terrestrial Ecosystems Project of the International Geosphere-Biosphere Program for nine years.

Peter Williams is the Chief Technology Officer, Big Green Innovations, at IBM, and an IBM Distinguished Engineer. His focus areas include resilience to natural disasters and chronic stresses, and 'smarter cities', with special reference to water management. He has had a major role in developing the intellectual foundation for IBM's Smarter Planet and Smarter Cities initiatives, and in identifying and integrating their technological components. Williams is a visiting lecturer on smarter cities and communities at Stanford University. His PhD was awarded by the School of Management at the University of Bath, England, in 1986.

Bibliography

2030 Water Resources Group (2012). "Charting Our Water Future." Available at: http://www.2030wrg.org/publication/charting-our-water-future/.

Ashoka (2012). "Ashoka Changemakers Launch Global Competition for Social Intrapreneurship." Press release, 26 September. Available at: https://www.ashoka.org/changemakers-launch-global-competition.

Barrow, E. (2013). "Retrofitting Resilience to the Shinyanga Landscape Restoration" (draft case study). IUCN Commission on Ecosystem Management, Gland, Switzerland.

Beck, M.W., et al. (2011). "Oyster Reefs at Risk Globally and Recommendations for Ecosystem Revitalization." *Bioscience* 61: 107-116.

Beinhocker, E. (2006). *The Origin of Wealth: Evolution, Complexity, and the Radical Remaking of Economics*. Boston: Harvard Business School Press.

Benedict, M.A., and E.T. McMahon (2002). "Green Infrastructure: Smart Conservation for the 21st Century." *Renewable Resources Journal* 20(3): 12-17.

Benedict, M.A., and E.T. McMahon (2006). *Green Infrastructure: Linking Landscapes and Communities*. Washington, DC: Island Press.

Bertalanffy, Ludwig von (1969) *General System Theory: Foundations, Development, Applications* George Braziller Inc.

Bohm, David (2002). *Wholeness and the Implicate Order*. New York: Routledge.

Boonstra, W.W. (2010). "Banking in Times of Crisis: The Case of Rabobank." In *The Quest for Stability: The View of Financial Institutions*, ed. Morten Balling, Jan Marc Berk and Marc-Olivier Strauss-Kahn. A joint publication with De Nederlandsche Bank and Rabobank, SUERF Study 2010/3.

Bortoft, Henri (1996). *The Wholeness of Nature – Goethe's Way of Science*. Edinburgh: Floris Books.

Calvache, A. (2009). *East Cauca Valley Water Fund*. The Nature Conservancy, Natural Capital Project.

City of New York, The (2013). *PlaNYC: A Stronger, More Resilient New York*. New York. Available at: http://www.nyc.gov/html/sirr/html/report/report.shtml.

Colander, D., and Kupers, R. (2014). *Complexity and the Art of Public Policy – Changing Society from the Bottom-Up*. Princeton: Princeton University Press.

Davis, C., and Farrelly, M. (2009). *Demonstration Projects: Case Studies from South East Queensland, Australia. National Urban Water Governance Programme*. Clayton, Victoria, Australia. Available at: http://www.waterforliveability.org.au/wp-content/uploads/demo_proj_se_qld.pdf.

Dietz, T., E. Ostrom, and P.C. Stern (2003). "The Struggle to Govern the Commons." *Science* 302: 1907-1912.

DiMuro, J.L., Guertin, F.M., Helling, R.K. Perkins, J.L. and Romer, S. (forthcoming 2014). "A Financial and Environmental Analysis of Constructed Wetlands for Industrial Waste Water Treatment." *Journal of Industrial Ecology.* doi: 10.1111/jiec.12129.

Dobbs, R., et al. (2011). *Resource Revolution: Meeting the World's Energy, Materials, Food and Water Needs*. McKinsey Global Institute. Available at: http://www.mckinsey.com/features/resource_revolution.

Dunn Cavelty, M., et al. (2011). "Using Scenarios to Assess Risks: Examining Trends in the Public Sector." CRN Report, Focal Report 5, Center for Security Studies (CSS), ETH Zürich.

Economics of Climate Adaptation Working Group (2009). *Shaping Climate-Resilient Development: A Framework for Decision-making.* Available at: http://ec.europa.eu/development/icenter/repository/ECA_Shaping_Climate_Resilent_Development.pdf.

Eggers, W.D., and P. MacMillan (2013). *The Solution Revolution: How Business, Government and Social Enterprises Are Teaming Up to Solve Society's Toughest Problems.* Boston: Harvard Business Review Press.

Ensor, Josie (2011). "Unilever's Polman Hits Out at City's Short-term Culture." *The Telegraph.* 5 July. Available at http://www.telegraph.co.uk/finance/newsbysector/retailandconsumer/8617022/Unilevers-Polman-hits-out-at-Citys-short-term-culture.html.

Entergy, America's Wetland Foundation, America's Energy Coast, Swiss Re (2010). "Building a Resilient Energy Gulf Coast: Executive Report." Available at: http://media.swissre.com/documents/Entergy_study_exec_report_20101014.pdf.

EPA (2010). *Green Infrastructure Case Studies: Municipal Policies for Managing Stormwater with Green Infrastructure.* EPA Office of Wetlands, Oceans and Watersheds. Washington, DC: US Environmental Protection Agency. Available at: http://www.epa.gov/owow/NPS/lid/gi_case_studies_2010.pdf.

European Parliament (2013). "On the Contribution of Cooperatives to Overcoming the Crisis." Committee on Industry, Research and Energy, 12 June. Available at: http://www.europarl.europa.eu/sides/getDoc.do?type=REPORT&reference=A7-2013-0222&language=EN.

Fiksel, J. (2010). "Evaluating Supply Chain Sustainability," *Chemical Engineering Progress* 106(5): 28-38.

Fox, Karyn M. (2012). *Resilience in Action: Adaptive Governance for Subak, Rice Terraces and Water Temples in Bali, Indonesia.* PhD thesis, University of Arizona.

Gell-Mann, Murray (1995). *The Quark and the Jaguar: Adventures in the Simple and the Complex.* New York: St. Martin's Press.

Gervetz, E., D. Goodrich, D. Semmens and C. Enquist (2012). "Case Study: Climate Impacting Fire Risk, Water Supply, Recreation and Flood Risk in the Western US Forests." The Nature Conservancy. Unpublished.

Goldman, R.B. (2010). *Water Funds: Protecting Watersheds for Nature and People.* The Nature Conservancy.

Gunderson, L., and C.S. Holling (2001). *Panarchy: Understanding Transformations in Systems of Humans and Nature*, Washington, DC: Island Press.

Habegger, B. (2009). "Factsheet: Identifikation von Risiken." *CRN Report.* Zürich: Center for Security Studies.

Hamel, G. and L. Välikangas (2003). "The Quest for Resilience." *Harvard Business Review*, September. Available at: http://hbr.org/2003/09/the-quest-for-resilience/ar/1 .

Higginson, N., and H. Vredenburg (2010). "Collaborating for Sustainability: Strategic Knowledge Networks, Natural Resource Management and Regional Development." *International Journal of Sustainable Economy* 2(3).

Hollings, C.S. (1973). "Resilience and Stability of Ecological Systems," *Annual Review of Ecology and Systematics.*

Homer-Dixon, T. (2000). *The Ingenuity Gap: Can We Solve the Problems of the Future?* Toronto: Vintage.

Homer-Dixon, T. (2006). *The Upside of Down: Catastrophe, Creativity and the Renewal of Civilization*. Toronto: Random House.

Huston, L., and N. Sakkab (2006). "Connect and Develop: Inside Procter & Gamble's New Model for Innovation." *Harvard Business Review*, March. Available at: http://hbr.org/2006/03/connect-and-develop-inside-procter-gambles-new-model-for-innovation/ar/1.

Ignatius, A. (2011). "Shaking Things Up at Coca-Cola: An Interview with Muhtar Kent." *Harvard Business Review*, October. Available at http://hbr.org/2011/10/shaking-things-up-at-coca-cola/.

International Federation of Red Cross and Red Crescent Societies (2011). *Breaking the Waves: Impact Analysis of Coastal Afforestation for Disaster Risk Reduction in Viet Nam.* Geneva: International Federation of Red Cross and Red Crescent Societies.

IPS (2012). *Prism Scenarios.* From http://ips-prism-an-immersive-arts-experience-national-library-board/; http://www.ips.sg/prism/scenarios.html.

IRI (2010). *HARITA IRI Report to Oxfam America: Final Report for IRI MIEL Planning & Technical Support for HARITA Micro-Insurance Pilot USA 536/09, June 2010.* New York: International Research Institute for Climate and Society. Available at: http://iri.columbia.edu/docs/publications/TR10-08_HARITA%20Report%20to%20OXFAM%20June2010.pdf.

Jankel, N. (2011). *Radical (Re)invention: Why There Are So Few Breakthrough Social Innovations and 20 Recommendations to Overcome the Barriers.* White Paper. Available at: http://jbctm.files.wordpress.com/2011/05/radicalreinvention.pdf.

Jones, M., and N. Christoffersen (2013). "Restoration of Forest Systems and Rural Livelihoods in Wallowa County, Oregon: A Partial Resilience Assessment of a Work in Progress." Draft case study. IUCN Commission on Ecosystem Management. Gland, Switzerland.

Kaplan, R.S., and A. Mikes. (2012a). "J.P. Morgan's Loss: Bigger Than 'Risk Management'." *HBR Blog Network.* 11 June. Available at: http://blogs.hbr.org/cs/2012/05/jp_morgans_loss_bigger_than_ri.html.

Kaplan, R.S., and A. Mikes (2012b). "Managing Risks: A New Framework." *Harvard Business Review*, June. Available at: http://hbr.org/2012/06/managing-risks-a-new-framework/ar/1.

Kaznierczak, A., and J. Carter (2010). *Adaptation to Climate Change Using Green and Blue Infrastructure.* Manchester: University of Manchester Press.

Koster, R. (2005). *Theory of Fun for Game Design.* Scottsdale, AZ: Paraglyph Press.

Kotter, J.P. (1996). *Leading Change.* Boston: Harvard Business School Press.

Krchnak, K.M. (2011). "Putting Nature in the Nexus: Investing in Natural Infrastructure to Advance Water-Energy-Food Security." In *The Water, Energy and Food Security Nexus – Solutions for the Green Economy.* Bonn: The Nature Conservancy.

Kroeger, T. (2012). "Oyster Reef Restoration in the Northern Gulf of Mexico: Assessing Economic Rationales for Large-Scale Restoration Efforts." TEEB 2012 Conference, Leipzig.

Kroeger, T., Guannel, G (2014). Fishery enhancement, coastal protection and water quality services provided by two restored Gulf of Mexico oyster reefs, in: Ninan, K.N. (Ed.), *Valuing Ecosystem Services - Methodological Issues and Case Studies.* Edward Elgar Publishing, Cheltenham, UK.

Lansing, J.S. (2006). *Perfect Order.* Princeton: Princeton University Press.

Lansing, J.S., and Kremer, J.N. (1993). "Emergent Properties of Balinese Water Temple Networks: Coadaptation on a Rugged Fitness Landscape." *American Anthropologist*, new series, 95(1): 97-114.

Martin-Breen, P., and J.M. Anderies (2011). "Resilience: A Literature Review." Rockefeller Foundation. Available at: http://www.rockefellerfoundation.org/blog/resilience-literature-review.

McKinsey & Company (2012). "Winning the $30 trillion Decathlon." McKinsey & Company. Available at: http://www.mckinsey.com/features/30_trillion_decathlon.

Natural Resources Defense Council, EKO Asset Management Partners and The Nature Conservancy (2013). *Creating Clean Water Cash Flows: Developing Private Markets for Green Stormwater Infrastructure in Philadelphia.* Natural Resources Defense Council. Available at: http://www.nature.org/ourinitiatives/regions/northamerica/unitedstates/pennsylvania/pa-stormwater-report.pdf.

Nature Conservancy, The, and Dow (2013). *2013 Annual Progress Report.* Available at: http://www.dow.com/sustainability/pdf/2013_Nature_Conservancy_Annual_Progress%20.pdf.

Nisen, Max (2013). "Samsung Has a Totally Different Strategy from Apple, and It's Working Great." *Business Insider,* 15 March. Available at: http://www.businessinsider.com/samsung-corporate-strategy-2013-3.

Opperman, J. (n.d.). "From Reoperation of Dams to Reoperation of Systems." The Nature Conservancy. Unpublished.

Ostrom, E. (2005). *Understanding Institutional Diversity.* Princeton: Princeton University Press.

Ostrom, E. (2010). "Beyond Markets and States: Polycentric Governance of Complex Economic Systems." *American Economic Review* 100: 1-33.

Padilla, P.H.M. (2011). "Fondo Agua por la Vida y la Sostenibilidad: Valle Geographico del Rio Cauca." ASOCANA.

Perrow, C. (1999). *Normal Accidents: Living with High-Risk Technologies.* Princeton: Princeton University Press.

Polman, Paul (2013). "Young People, A Sustainable Future Can Be Yours, Make Your Work Count." *Forbes,* 19 February. Available at: http://www.forbes.com/sites/ashoka/2013/09/02/paul-polman-young-people-a-sustainable-future-can-be-yours-make-your-work-count/.

PwC (2011). "Black Swans Turn Grey: The Transformation of the Risk Landscape." In Risk Practices: Navigating the Enterprise through a World Beset by Uncertainty. Available at: http://pdf.pwc.co.uk/risk-practices-black-swans-turn-grey-the-transformation-of-the-risk-landscape.pdf.

PwC, in association with SSEE at Oxford University (2012). *Prospering in an Era of Uncertainty: The Case for Resilience.* Available at: http://pwc.blogs.com/files/the-case-for-resilience1.pdf.

PwC, University of Southern California and London Business School (2013). *PwC's NextGen: A Global Generational Study – Evolving Talent Strategy to Match the New Workforce Reality – Summary and Compendium of Fndings.* Available at: http://www.pwc.com/en_GX/gx/hr-management-services/pdf/pwc-nextgen-study-2013.pdf.

Ramos, A., S. Benitez and A. Calvache (2012). *Fondos de Agua: Conservado la Infraestructura Verde: Gúia de deseño, creación y operación.* The Nature Conservancy, Fundación Femsa, Banco Interamericano de Desarrollo.

Reeves, M., and M. Deimler (2011). "Adaptability: The New Competitive Advantage," *Harvard Business Review,* July. Available at: http://hbr.org/2011/07/adaptability-the-new-competitive-advantage/ar/1.

Regional Plan Association and Siemens. (2013). *Toolkit for Resilient Cities, Case Study: New York City Electrical Grid.* Available at: (http://w3.siemens.com/topics/global/en/sustainable-cities/resilience/Documents/pdf/Toolkit_for_Resilient%20Cities_NY_Case_Study.pdf.

Reinmoeller, P., and N. van Baardwijk (2005). "The Link between Diversity and Resilience." *MIT Sloan Management Review* 46(4): 61-64.

Rockström, J., et al. (2009) "A Safe Operating Space for Humanity." *Nature* 461: 472-475.

Rocky Mountain Institute (2010). "Carsharing members (North America and Europe) and Projected Growth." Available at: http://www.rmi.org/RFGraph-Carsharing_members_and_projected_growth.

Rotterdam School of Management (2012), *Onderzoeksrapport topsectoren – Sociale innovatie doorslaggevend voor topsectoren.* Available at: http://www.rsm.nl/fileadmin/Images_NEW/News_Images/2014/ONDERZOEKSRAPPORT_TOPSECTOREN.pdf.

Scheffer, M. (2009). *Critical Transitions in Nature and Society.* Princeton Studies in Complexity. Princeton: Princeton University Press.

Schmuki, A. (2009). "The Role of a Global Organisation in Triggering Social Learning – Insights from a Case Study of a World Heritage Cultural Landscape Nomination in Bali." Stockholm Resilience Center.

Senge, P. (1990) *The fifth discipline - The Art & Practice of The Learning Organization.* (Currency Doubleday).

Sheffi, Y. (2007). *The Resilient Enterprise: Overcoming Vulnerability for Competitive Advantage.* Cambridge, MA: MIT Press Books.

Shell (2013), "New Lens Scenarios – A Shift in Perspective for a World in Transition." Available at: http://s01.static-shell.com/content/dam/shell-new/local/corporate/Scenarios/Downloads/Scenarios_newdoc.pdf.

Starr, R., J. Newfrock and M. Delurey (2003). "Enterprise Resilience: Managing Risks in the Networked Economy." *Strategy + Business* 30: 70-79. Available at: http://www.strategy-business.com/article/8375?pg=all.

Styles, Kirsty (2012). "Community Energy Cooperatives Take on the 'Big Six.'" *Wired* (UK), 22 October. Available at: http://www.wired.co.uk/news/archive/2012-10/22/community-energy-initiatives.

Swearingen, Jake (2008). "Great Intrapreneurs in Business History." *Moneywatch*, 10 April. Available at: http://www.cbsnews.com/news/great-intrapreneurs-in-business-history/.

Swiss Re (2009). *Country Risk Management: Making Societies More Resilient.* Zurich: Swiss Reinsurance.

Taleb, N.N. (2007). *The Black Swan: The Impact of the Highly Improbable.* New York: random House.

Tallis, H., and A. Calvache (2011). *Improving Conservation Investment Returns for People and Nature in the East Cauca Valley, Columbia.* The Nature Conservancy. Natural Capital Project.

Turnbull, M., C.L. Sterrett and A. Hilleboe (2013). *Toward Resilience: A Guide to Disaster Risk Reduction and Climate Change Adaptation.* Warwickshire: Practical Action Publishing.

Välikangas, L. (2004). "Four Steps to Corporate Resilience." *Strategy + Business* 35. Available at: http://www.strategy-business.com/article/04215?gko=908d9.

Van Dijk, G. (1999). "Evolution of Business Structure and Entrepreneurship of Cooperatives in the Horti- and Agribusiness." *LTA* 4/99: 471-483. Available at: http://lta.hse.fi/1999/4/lta_1999_04_a7.pdf.

Voice of America (2010). "South African Business Tackles HIV/AIDS", *Voice of America*, 15 June. Available at: http://www.voanews.com/content/south-african-business-tackles-hivaids-96470209/154918.html. the head of Shell

Waldrop, Mitchell (1992). *Complexity: The Emerging Science at the Edge of Order and Chaos*. New York: Simon & Schuster.

Walker, B. (2013). "What Is Resilience?" *Project Syndicate*, 5 July. Available at http://www.project-syndicate.org/commentary/what-is-resilience-by-brian-walker.

Walker, B., N. Abel, J.M. Anderies and P. Ryan (2009). "Resilience, Adaptability, and Transformability in the Goulburn-Broken Catchment, Australia." *Ecology & Society* 14(1): 1-24.

Walker, B., and D. Salt (2006). *Resilience Thinking: Sustaining Ecosystems and People in a Changing World*. Washington, DC: Island Press.

Walker, B. and D. Salt (2012). *Resilience Practice: Building Capacity to Absorb Disturbance and Maintain Function*. Washington, DC: Island Press.

Warner, A., J. Opperman and R. Pietrowsky (2011). "A Call to Enhance the Resiliency of the Nation's Water Management." *Journal of Water Resources Planning and Management* 137(4): 305-308.

Westley, F., et al. (2011). "Tipping toward Sustainability: Emerging Pathways of Transformation." *Ambio* 40: 762-780.

Wilkinson, A., and R. Kupers (2013). "Living in the Futures." *Harvard Business Review*, May. Available at: http://hbr.org/2013/05/living-in-the-futures/ar/1.

Wilkinson, A., and R. Kupers (2014). *The Essence of Corporate Scenarios: Learning from the Shell Experience*. Amsterdam: Amsterdam University Press.

Wilkinson, R., and K. Pickett (2010). *The Spirit level*. Penguin Books.

Zolli, A., and A.M. Healy (2012). *Resilience: Why Things Bounce Back*. London: Headline Publishing Group.

Index